New Product Development _Checklists_

N T C B U S I N E S S B O O K S

New Product Development Checklists

HF 5415.153 .G77 1991

PROVEN CHECKLISTS FOR DEVELOPING NEW PRODUCTS FROM MISSION TO MARKET

George Gruenwald

NTC Business Books
a division of *NTC Publishing Group* • Lincolnwood, Illinois USA

Library of Congress Cataloging-in-Publication Data

Gruenwald, George.
 New product development checklists / George Gruenwald.
  p.   cm.
 ISBN 0-8442-3217-3
 1. New products. 2. Product management. I. Title.
HF5415.153.G77 1991
658.5'75—dc20   90-43722

Published by NTC Business Books, a division of NTC Publishing Group,
4255 West Touhy Avenue, Lincolnwood (Chicago), Illinois 60646-1975 U.S.A.
© 1991 by George Gruenwald. All rights reserved.
1 2 3 4 5 6 7 8 9 VP 9 8 7 6 5 4 3 2 1

For Corrine
—and for all the new products we've created together

Contents

Contents

Foreword

Dedication to quality is the single most powerful factor that distinguishes those organizations that stay at the top of their industries from their competitors. And in no area of business is quality as critical to success as in the development and marketing of new products and services.

This commitment to excellence is at the heart of George Gruenwald's new book. In his extensive and proven system of checklists, he provides a model which any organization can use to plot a course for the development of new products that will be leaders in their class.

Market successes are rarely achieved overnight, no matter how innovative the ideas behind them. Surer guarantees are a thorough understanding of the customer for whom a new product is created, attention to detail at every stage of its planning and production, and—perhaps most important—open lines of communication among everyone involved in the project. George Gruenwald's approach ensures that all these bases are covered—quality products and services follow.

Robert W. Galvin
Chairman of the Executive Committee and former CEO, Motorola Inc.

Preface

The future of any enterprise, from the largest multinational corporation to the smallest start-up company, depends on the skill with which it develops new products and services and brings them to the market. This means that new product development is one of the most exciting—and the most frightening—of challenges that forward-looking businesses face. While few experiences come close to the genuine ecstasy of watching new product ideas come to life and take off in the marketplace, mistakes are costly and can weaken the organization as a whole.

In his new book, George Gruenwald takes you by the hand and walks you safely through the minefield of new product development. I recommend you use his comprehensive system of checklists as a working model for setting objectives, and for planning and implementing new product or service ideas. Not only will it help you ensure that all the players are in place and that all opportunities are explored before money and time are invested in new product plans, it will guarantee that no essential steps are missed during the development process.

This is the best, most practical planning guide I have seen. Use it to transform your new product ideas into profitable market successes.

Lewis W. Lehr
Former Chairman of the Board and CEO, 3M

Introduction

Upfront knowledge is the key to new product success.

The discipline of the new product checklist is to be certain that no consideration is overlooked. It is not to assure that all are implemented.

Countless new product failures are attributable to missed, ignored, misplaced, or purposely gap-jumped essential steps or information. Almost every flop finds its cause in something which appears obvious after the fact and, in many cases, obvious in the very early, least-costly phases of development. The early, regularly-modified detailed perspective is what a comprehensive checklist system provides.

"The stage of development of any product or technology is not susceptible to measurement as a characteristic of the product. It can only be established by comparison with some arbitrary scale, i.e., by association with one of a set of defined 'states' laid out along a time axis. The suitability of any such scale is given by the convenience of its application and by the breadth of its acceptance."[1]

Successes can come from instinct, from inspiration. Far more likely, however, successes come from knowing which *t*s to cross, which *i*s to dot—and which to ignore. But you can only ignore them if you recognize them.

Therefore, it is mandatory to review all possible aspects of the program at its inception—and to reassess continually . . . as the program moves along to its destiny. This destiny, in most cases, is termination—as early as possible, in order to make the precious human, time and financial resources available for more promising projects.

It is the purpose of this book to provide a comprehensive listing and suggested evaluation or assignment methods for each key new product development step from corporate charter to commercialization—from mission to market.

Thus, the purpose is to amplify your wisdom in planning and in revising the time line, deployment of resources, budgeting, authorizations—all aspects of the process. How you utilize the checklist is a matter of judgment. Some

---

[1]From an unpublished document by George P. Lewitt, Office of Energy-Related Inventions, National Institute of Standards and Technology (formerly National Bureau of Standards), U.S. Department of Commerce. The quote is taken from the New Product Stages of Development Project Description of NIST/NSPE (National Society of Professional Engineers), of which this book's author was a corresponding Task Group member. Quoted with permission.

will merely use it to see whether all aspects are considered. Others will use it for assignments, priorities and reviews. Some will elaborate it with a weighted scoring system. Others may implement a more complex mathematical equation system, easily adaptable to computer programming.

Because new product development can originate from so many sources within the company, trade, outside inventors, consultants and even tangential suppliers, the checklist must be an eclectic one subject to staging by the initiating knowledge base and the control source. This control is determined by the mission: a major corporate charter change, a new business category entry, a basic research breakthrough or requirement, or the more usual market-driven or applied-technology driven force to enhance existing momentum, to increase share or as a defensive reaction to competition or customer change, including attitudinal, behavioral and regulatorial change.

The checklists are designed to assign responsibilities, and to indicate levels of same. Additionally, they may be modified to also include weighting of importance and time lines, due dates, etc. The checklists may also be modified to apply to varying levels of complex science-driven needs in high-risk areas, as well as to simple line-extensions of establishing products using applicable industry standard R&D, manufacturing and marketing. Where possible, if a proprietary technology can leverage an innovation, this is a key factor in the decision process. The overall benefit of the checklist system is to be certain not to overlook serious attention to any phase of new product development.

Each phase in the new product checklist array is herein treated in a manner which the author has found effective. Illustrative examples are provided. The term "new products" includes new *services* in its definition.

The checklist approach is a proven one, developed and used by the author as a new products brand and advertising manager, as a founder of one of the first new products consultancies (including sales and distribution resources), as a founding member of a new products-driven advertising agency, as chief executive of another and as new products management consultant to many of the world's largest corporations. This opportunity development experience ranges across most major businesses, including consumer, professional and institutional products and services. Additionally, voluntary contributions to innovation are made in the public broadcasting, scientific, engineering, medical, arts and educational fields. Current commentary on new products appears in *Marketing News,* a publication of the American Marketing Association.

Few, if any, practitioners have been through the new product process from so many managerial perspectives, in so many fields, working with so many industry leaders and specialists over so many years—and with so many successes.

The seminal checklist for the elaborate working system in this book was developed in the 1950s, when a simplified version was published. Following its success, various revisions have appeared in the business press. Most recently, a summary version was incorporated in my earlier work, *New Product Development.*[2]

---

[2]George Gruenwald, *New Product Development,* NTC Publishing Group, Lincolnwood, 1985.

Pick Your Own Playing Field

BEFORE YOU START

Maybe you're an entrepreneur with lots of ideas.

Maybe you're a company executive who needs new products or services to stay in the forefront, to get ahead, or, at least, to hold the line.

Maybe you're thinking of diversifying an established product line.

Maybe you know exactly where you are and what you want to do.

Whatever your plans, this introductory section will help you review your current business situation and will help you define realistic future objectives—both essential first steps in any new product development program.

As history tells us that most new products fail for reasons which may have been apparent at or near the outset, an initial review is critical. It's important to know—at least in a general sense—where you are and where you want to go. Moreover, it's important that all involved in initiating, developing, evaluating, producing or marketing any new product understand the objectives.

The checklists illustrated in this section are the starting point for planning the new product development process. They provide, in an easy-to-use format, a summary of the major aspects you will need to consider throughout any new business activity. And if your business operates in a competitive environment—as is most likely the case—it's best to pick your own playing field before you start.

In picking that playing field, there are three essential beginning elements:

Today's reality—what you are (and are not), as defined in a *Corporate Charter*.

Today's ambition—where you want to go, as defined in a *Corporate Objective* statement.

Today's plan—how you are going to get there, as defined in a *Strategic Mission* statement.

If you have any of these statements on the record, the checklist formats will help to review and determine if anything has been overlooked or needs revision.

If any of these statements are not clearly defined, the checklists will help you frame comprehensive, action-oriented direction.

If you are using the checklist as an individual, subjective weighting of each aspect is sufficient.

If a group is evaluating the checklist, then you may wish to use a weighting method to compare and integrate or average the different evaluations in arriving at clearly expressed statements of charter, objective and the strategy to achieve it.

For a small, entrepreneurial start-up company, the related checklists help amplify the perspective and provide a means by which few aspects of the business will be overlooked at the beginning. For larger, established businesses, the checklists can help gather a variety of perspectives from staff. This forces the responsible ultimate decision maker to evaluate each viewpoint as it relates to the overall quest of management. In all cases, the checklist approach serves as a necessary discipline for the formation of an actionable business focus.

What Do We Mean by Corporate?

The first step in planning for new product development is to define the organization's current business status, and to identify future goals. One proven approach is developing in written form the organization's Corporate Charter and statement of Corporate Objective. Let's begin by clarifying exactly what we mean by *corporate*.

The word *corporate*, as used here, describes the business unit responsible for the assignment at hand. In some cases, for example, it may be the entire, single-centered company. In others, it might be a specific division or subsidiary of the company. It may be those who work on a particular brand, or it may be a special task force. Corporate, then, describes any general organizational concept that is the focus of the assignment and that defines its boundaries or limits. If you're an entrepreneur, the focus may be your own invention. If you run your own business, it may be limited only by your wish to make a dream come true. In most organizations, however, more than one person or department is involved, each with different areas of expertise and varying levels of responsibility.

Where to begin?

It depends on where the driving force comes from. In some companies, this involves either waiting for "the lab" to come up with something new before the project gets rolling, or simply saying, "Let's turn it over to marketing."

The practitioner knows there is no regular order of things. New product veterans know that new ideas do indeed come from anywhere, know that a free and unfettered climate works best, know that a mutuality of interests dictates that the creative people in the lab, in marketing, in management, in outside services should start together, with all background information provided. Then, let them work in their own best styles.

It's important to do the more detailed work in the conceptual stage, the thinking-about-it stage. "That's the inexpensive time to make changes, before you start engineering and manufacturing," says recently retired Ford Motor Co. Chairman Donald Petersen.[1]

The Corporate Charter and Corporate Objective, therefore, reflect the perspectives, input, capabilities, and responsibilities of a wide range of influences and functions within the organization.

If your organization has already formulated a written Charter and statement of Corporate Objective, review these and make sure that nothing has been overlooked or needs revision. The following sections and the first checklist will help.

FIRST, THE CORPORATE CHARTER

The Corporate Charter is the basic starting document for planning any new business activity. It reflects the clearest possible strategic business focus. When beginning a new product project, a fundamental question is: Does this fit the Corporate Charter? The mission's advisability depends on the answer.

The Corporate Charter is a short, clear statement of what the company's current business situation *is* and what it *is not*. It summarizes, for example, the products manufactured and the ways in which these are marketed and distributed. It also gives a brief overview of the organization's strengths and weaknesses.

Most Corporate Charters seem to be mere hymns to motherhood and the flag—they are often too vague and idealistic to be of any practical use. If this sounds like your Corporate Charter, the first thing to do is to insist on a rewrite. Force yourself and your company to think it through thoroughly and come up with something better. Look at it as the necessary starting point for any successful new product program. A specific, refined, and periodically redefined Corporate Charter will set the course.

Case Example: Rewriting the Corporate Charter

To illustrate what your Corporate Charter should be and what it should include, here's a fictional example and a subsequent rewrite:

"ABC Corporation is in the business of making and marketing the best quality nutritional supplements at the lowest cost and with the most attractive selling price."

---

[1]*Forbes* magazine, August 20, 1990.

Excellent. But for new product planning purposes, it needs detailed modification. Here's the first redraft:

"ABC Corporation is a manufacturer of nutritional supplements: vitamins, minerals, enzymes, amino acids, emulsifiers, digestive aid fibers, and various combinations thereof. These products are marketed to physicians, nutritionists, and pharmacies. Products are also sold through direct marketing through mail to end users, the only public promotion used. The Company uses limited professional journal advertising. The corporate name is carried on all items, together with accepted generic term descriptors. The Company uses stock packaging with plain labeling. Distribution is through direct mail to the professional and pharmacy trades, primarily in Massachusetts and contiguous states.

"The Company has state-of-the-art manufacturing and reliable, competitively-priced suppliers, which makes possible the most attractive selling price.

"It has a limited area trade selling force. The Company does not have consumer-oriented expertise, nor major funding for marketing communications efforts.

"The Company is profitable, growth-oriented, conservative, and privately held."

Make sure that your draft Corporate Charter is similarly clear and comprehensive.

SECOND, THE CORPORATE OBJECTIVE

Whereas the Corporate Charter clarifies in general terms a company's current business situation, the statement of Corporate Objective shows exactly what that company wants to become. It details realistic objectives that describe what the company intends to be, for example, in terms of product development, and marketing and distribution plans. It should also outline exactly what the company does *not* intend to do or become.

Case Example: Writing the Statement of Corporate Objective

With the refined, detailed Corporate Charter in hand, this Corporate Objective was composed for ABC Corporation:

"Within five years we will expand our product line in our strongest East Coast acceptance areas. This will include development and addition of a new line of specially formulated skin and hair products to be marketed to the Company's existing product base.

"At the same time, we will experimentally develop and test acceptance of pet nutrition items, which we will offer to established direct mail prospects and to veterinarians, pet care and pet supply outlets in several markets where the Company's nutritional products sell best.

"We will support the pet nutrition line with appropriate marketing communications, including special professional, trade, and general news releases, and expert-endorser personal appearances on test-area radio and television news and interview shows.

"We will test specially-retained sales/distribution services qualified for the pet-care field. We will develop and offer point-of-purchase merchandising materials and incentives. There will be no general media advertising."

Evaluating the Corporate Charter and the Corporate Objective

Now, no Corporate Charter or Corporate Objective should be a one person show—all personnel or departments involved in the business functions they describe or the objectives they set should understand and support both statements. If, after completing the process, there is lack of agreement, the majority recommendation should be qualified by recognizing the differences and by referring them to the next level of management for resolution. At the outset, all will not agree on what should be included or how this should be stated. So, gather the forces. The next step is to select the most astute, articulate persons from each department of the organization. They will be assigned to evaluate the draft Corporate Charter and statement of Corporate Objective and will suggest ways in which these might be improved to better reflect the current business situation and reasonable business objectives.

Use Checklist 1.1 to elicit from these key people judgmental evaluations of the two documents as they currently stand. It is a short questionnaire that is designed to prompt subjective viewpoints. It is divided into two parts: the top half requests perspectives on the Corporate Charter—what the company's current business situation is and what it is not; and the bottom half asks for each representative's view on what the company intends, and what it does not intend.

There should be plenty of room on the checklist for evaluators to explain their comments, and this should be encouraged, particularly where evaluators recommend that the statements need to be reworded. Ask them, if necessary, to add an additional sheet to explain their criticisms or suggestions.

This subjective approach works best because it encourages a wider range of thinking than would be possible, for example, on a numerical questionnaire. This allows for new and different perspectives on the business situation and leads to better understanding and agreement.

You will note that Checklist 1.1 has narrow columns which evaluators use to indicate opinion (i.e. a checkmark after "Agree/Approve as Stated" indicates complete, uncritical acceptance of document being evaluated), whereas any checkmark in the narrow columns under the "Needs Rework" heading requires an explanation (i.e. a checkmark after "Too General'' is accompanied by this comment in the column at left: ''Implies international business—see appended note on negative implication''). It is necessary that each evaluator explain each ''Needs Rework'' checkmark. No appended elaborated, documented explanation is required in all cases, such as ''No longer true. Patent expired three months ago,'' etc.

The working model illustrated in Checklist 1.1 can be modified to suit your company's special needs. With it, you can accurately assess the whole organization's perspective on where you are and where you ought to be heading.

Goal-setting Parameters

Goal-setting Parameters

(See attached sheet and evaluate whether this represents clear, specific, detailed statements of current Corporate Charter and Corporate Objective, relating to all elements of the operation)

CORPORATE CHARTER

What My Company Is

_____

What My Company Is NOT

_____

What My Company Is GOOD at

_____

What My Company Is NOT Good at

_____

Is the Corporate Charter as written on the attached sheet an acceptable, understandable statement of the above?

_____

CORPORATE OBJECTIVE

What My Company INTENDS to Be

_____

What My Company Does NOT Intend to Be

_____

Is the Corporate Objective as written on the attached sheet an acceptable, understandable statement of the above?

_____

Evaluation by

Name _____

Department/Title _____

Agree/Approve as Stated _____						
Needs Rework Factually		Too Explicit		Too General		Other Reasons (see notes appended)

Interpreting Responses to Checklist 1.1

As questionaires/checklists are returned, make sure each person has filled in name, title, department and specialization. These details are important in assessing responses. Your evaluation system should recognize that each opinion is from a different perspective, from persons with different qualifications and levels of authority. You may choose to review appropriate personnel files to familiarize yourself with certain representative's roles in the company, years of service and outside experience.

The next step is for a knowledgeable, noninvolved senior executive to assess objectively the opinions of each evaluator. A weighting scale, for example, can be used which gives greater emphasis to comments made by experienced, well-informed personnel than to comments made by those who are not closely involved in a particular field or specialization. To illustrate, in assessing manufacturing strengths, the manufacturing manager's opinion will be of greater value than, say, the marketing chief's and should be weighted accordingly.

Use as straightforward a system as possible to weigh and compare responses. One simple method is to give values, say on a scale of 1 to 3, to each point on the checklist, and award marks in terms of each respondent's expertise. If, for example, a marketing specialist comments on marketing aspects of the statements, award his or her opinion a score of 3. If, however, the marketing specialist criticizes legal aspects of the statements, these comments may merit only a score of 1, as they are not based on expertise in that area. Nonetheless, the non-specialist perspective may provide valuable, otherwise overlooked insights.

You may want to make your weighting system more detailed, by evaluating on a scale of 1 to 10, or more simple by awarding straight + or − points. Whatever system you use, all that matters is that you are objective and consistent.

Case Example: Interpreting Responses

Let's look at examples of the information gathered by ABC Corporation in response to circulating a checklist based on the redrafted Corporate Charter and statement of Corporate Objective.

Our guru assigned to assessing each representative's report has several dozen evaluations coming in. He has already established criteria for assessing viewpoints on each element included on the questionnaire and compares responses with each individual's corporate history and experience. He has chosen a +/− weighting scale.

To see how this works, look at the two returned checklists in Exhibit 1.1. Two representatives—one from the R&D Department, one from

Exhibit 1.1. Assessing completed checklists

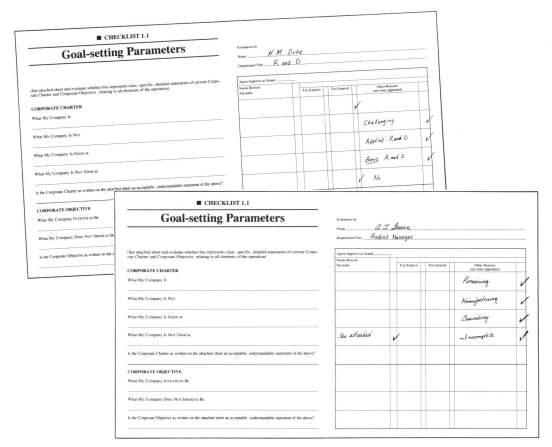

Product Management—have completed their evaluations of the Corporate Charter. Their opinions are assessed in conjunction with their performance records.

Our guru has assigned the same weight to each element on the checklist, but has given product manager Green's complete report special weight because she has worked in several areas of the company. In this case, our management guru has assigned the same weight to each element on the checklist. Product manager Green's report is given a plus score, because of her experience in different areas of the company. Mr. Duke, from R&D, is new to the company's specialization and has not been with the company long. Therefore, his R&D perspective gets special attention, whereas his views on other areas are scored neutral. His two R&D checks relate to his reasons for thinking the company's Corporate Charter is not "challenging" and that its R&D function has little devotion to basic research, as opposed to its close-in applied research. His appended comments make suggestions both supportive of his opinion and positively remedial, without sacrificing the short-range R&D programs.

THIRD, THE STRATEGIC MISSION

Now that all the comments and specific input have been weighed and utilized in the final drafts of approved Corporate Charter and Corporate Objective, it is necessary to formulate a concrete, directional, prioritized Strategic Mission Statement to guide new business and product development.

Checklist 1.2 includes all of the key elements generally necessary to form comprehensive, clearly directional guidelines to mission achievement. It spotlights both strengths at hand and the areas needing improvement to successfully activate the mission strategy.

The checklist is to be completed by representatives of all departments which will play a role at any time in the foreseeable history of the mission. The input from all will be taken into consideration by the highest-ranked working member of the development team, who will prepare the formal draft for submission to management for approval.

This draft, prior to submission, will serve as a weighted, priority checklist to be reviewed with the key input members of the checklist evaluators—those who will be responsible for the mission's activation into reality. Taking into account these comments, the team leader will submit the strategic mission statement to the top (funding) management for approval.

Whenever action is required by a major policy, line or overall operational office responsible for company activity, an asterisk (*) is indicated. To modify to fit your own situation, additional management checklist columns are provided.

The checklist has served to give a clear and accurate picture of every aspect of the organization's operations relating to the mission strategy, emphasizing those areas or departments that will be most closely involved in the new product development programs.

The checklist is comprehensive, including an evaluation of management, personnel, facilities and resources; a summary of proprietary and marketing strengths; details of financial status and market position; innovation requirements, and a complete business analysis. The checklist format also provides space for appended areas which may be unique to your specific business.

It is critical that the checklist you use accommodates all affected and affecting parties within your organization. Each business is built differently, whether it be maker, processor, builder, servicer or seller, or any combination of these. It will be made up of any number of different departments, each with a different function. Make sure that your checklist allows for input from all functions within your organization.

Notice how Checklist 1.2 is laid out. Each business function or department is listed in the column headings at the top of the page. There is room for you to add others. You can adapt, enlarge upon or change our suggested checkoffs that are listed on the left-hand side of the page. All that matters is that your checklist accommodates representatives from all elements of your business and allows each to participate in this early step in new product development. In this way, you cover all the bases. You can receive input both from those departments that are most closely involved in new product development, *and* from less likely sources. For example, the Medical Department—normally only concerned with employee health and safety—may have important insights into potential uses for a new product you are developing; marketing may know of a new, appropriate supplier, not utilized by Purchasing; R&D may suggest subcontracting some applied research early on, and opt to include the supplier in the early phases of development, and so on.

The main thing is: don't miss any bases. Get everyone involved. Get all the help you can from the start, and make the most of in-house resources and know-how. It is both essential now, and motivating for what's ahead.

The checklist is to be completed by representatives of all departments that will play a role at any time in the foreseeable future of the mission. The input from all will be taken into consideration by the highest-ranked member of the development team, who will prepare the formal draft for submission to management for approval. This draft, prior to submission, will serve as a weighted, priority checklist to be reviewed periodically with the key department representatives.

Here's an example of how one of the supervising parties in an organization used the checklist to denote each department's area of responsibility during an early phase of developing the Strategic Mission Statement (see Exhibit 1.2). He put a checkmark in each box where he felt it was essential that evaluation and suggestion by particular departments was needed. He put an *R* in each box where he designated overall responsibility for a particular activity.

Note that where he felt the checklist was not sufficiently comprehensive, he modified it to suit the organization's needs. He added "Contracted Lab" and "Ecology" under the R&D action area heading in the left-hand column, and added "Medical" and "Consultant" to the resource area on the top right. In this way, he brought the functions of outside suppliers as well as in-house departments into the checklist.

Case Example: Using the Strategic Mission Checklist

For ABC Corporation, the Strategic Mission Checklist quickly isolated areas on which different departments agreed and disagreed. This helped management sort out the different requirements for the skin/hair care goals set out in the Corporate Objective. Getting input from various

Exhibit 1.2.   Completing the Strategic Mission Checklist

■ CHECKLIST 1.2

Strategic Mission

Applicable to Corporate Objective Evaluation Areas:

- SHAREHOLDER COMMITMENT*
- MANAGEMENT/BOARD OF DIRECTORS' COMMITMENT*
- BASIC RESEARCH CAPABILITIES
- APPLIED RESEARCH CAPABILITIES
- RESEARCH & DEVELOPMENT AND/OR RESEARCH & ENGINEERING RESOURCES

  Staff

  Equipment

  Facilities

  Materials

  Other Resources

  Contracted Lab

  Ecology
- MANUFACTURING RESOURCES, IN RELATION TO INDUSTRY STANDARDS

  Staff

  Equipment

departments documented the need to revise initial goals. The checklist showed that, despite earlier, optimistic plans by management, the company's product experience in this area was limited. Once this was pointed out, management readily accepted a more targeted objective: to build on its product experience in nutrition and concentrate on developing a pet nutrition line. Even though new marketing skills were needed, this course of action fitted better with the company's existing strengths.

The checklist system can therefore supply detailed information on which new product decisions can be more reliably made. In the example above, corporate objectives were prioritized to reflect current technical, resource and market strengths.

The strategic mission checklist is especially valuable for multi-divisional, multi-departmental organizations with layered staff, or geographically-scattered functional bases. It is an information-gathering tool that can be used to help define current business status, areas of responsibility, and use of resources. It can help in evaluating new goals, and in discovering new opportunities.

By now, then, the stage is set. You have worked out a Corporate Charter which describes your business situation in terms which key personnel understand and agree. You have a statement of Corporate Objective which clarifies future goals and indicates, in general terms, the areas of new product development you plan to explore. Through the strategic mission checklist you have surveyed each element of your business operations and now know which objectives you can best realize.

The next step will be to determine where new opportunities lie, if the Strategic Mission Statement has been sufficiently persuasive in meriting the required business dedication.

Management will decide whether to move on to the next phase as proposed, or whether to extend/enlarge/embellish or accelerate the pursuit of the opportunity. Management may also decide to modify the definition of the strategic mission, in terms of timing, available budget and staff commitment.

If the proposal has not been sufficiently persuasive, management may elect to modify the program, or to suggest a substitute opportunity—or to abort the entire project. In the latter case, management may not have been persuaded by the particular strategic opportunity, and may instead elect to put the company's money behind a yet-to-be-determined opportunity. So, it's back to the drawing board . . . the search for the most appropriate strategic mission.

Should the signal be "full speed ahead," the Exploration for Opportunity phase begins.

Strategic Mission

Applicable to Corporate Objective Evaluation Areas:

- **SHAREHOLDER COMMITMENT***

- **MANAGEMENT/BOARD OF DIRECTORS' COMMITMENT***

- **BASIC RESEARCH CAPABILITIES**

- **APPLIED RESEARCH CAPABILITIES**

- **RESEARCH & DEVELOPMENT AND/OR RESEARCH & ENGINEERING RESOURCES**

  Staff

  Equipment

  Facilities

  Materials

  Other Resources

- **MANUFACTURING RESOURCES, IN RELATION TO INDUSTRY STANDARDS**

  Staff

  Equipment

  Facilities

  Materials

  Other Resources

- **PROPRIETARY STRENGTH**

  Patents (U.S., Foreign as applicable)

---

* Top management action/decision required

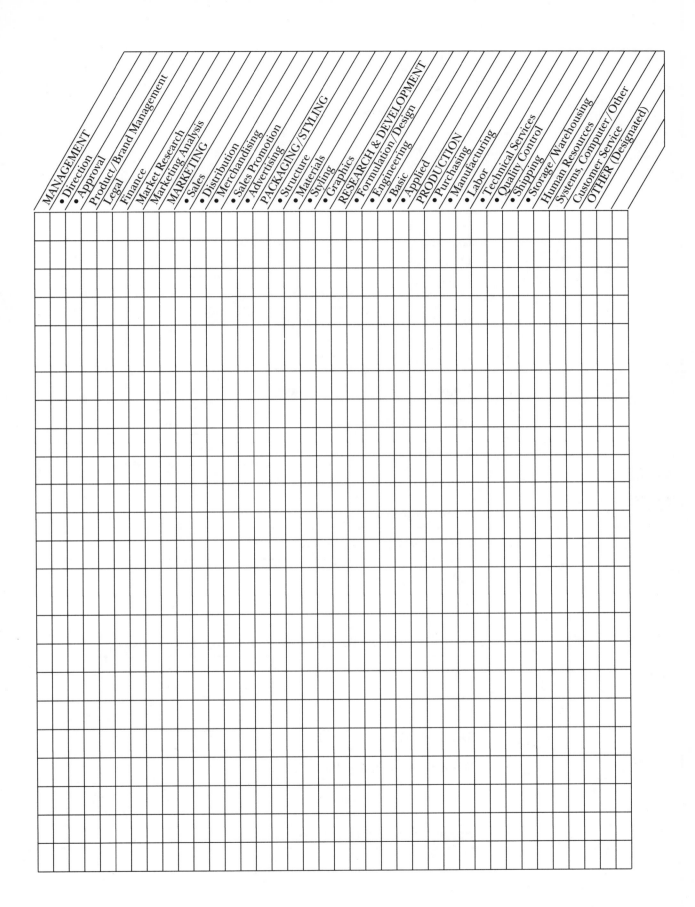

Trademarks

Copyrights

Secrecy Agreements (internal)

Secrecy Agreements (external)

Licensing (internal/external)

Captive Innovation Sources (including inventions)

Supplier Leverage/Control

Special Hires

Retained Outside Specialists, Consultants

Ownership Releases

Confidentiality Agreements

Other (indicate):

- **MARKETING STRENGTH (as defined by mission area)**

Selling

Distribution

Detailing at Points of Sale

Relative Advertising Power

Relative Promotional Power

Special Merchandising Power

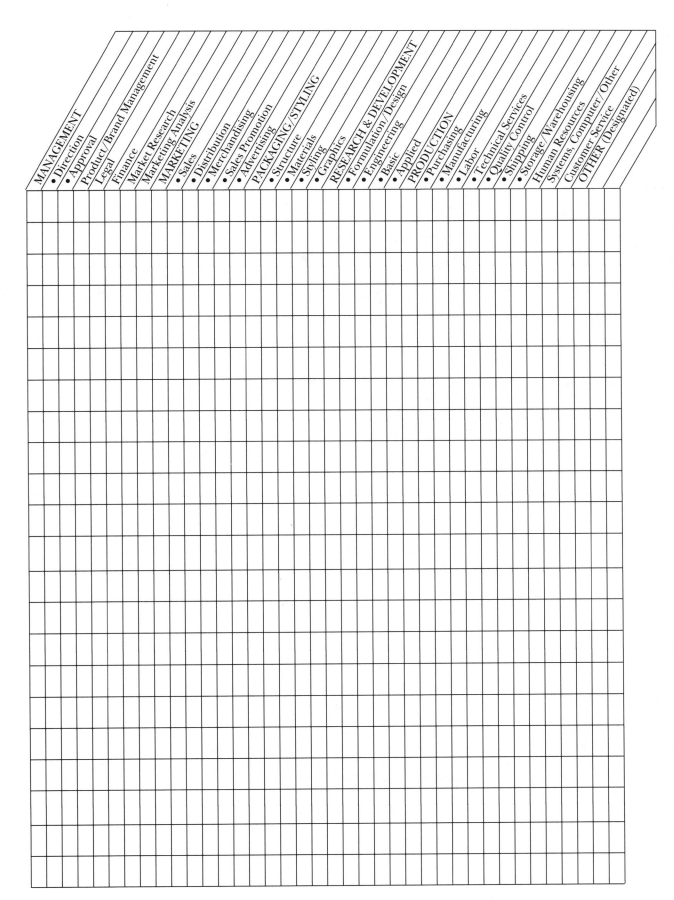

- **FINANCIAL APPROPRIATENESS**

Pricing Competitive

Margin Sufficient

Payout Timetable Realistic

Economies of Scale Yield

Unit Volume Goal (general, for corporate planning)

Dollar Value

 @ Factory

 @ Intermediate Wholesale/Markup Steps (including
 shelf-allowances, discounts, etc.)

 Retailer/End-Marketer Cost

 Purchaser/End-User Pricing

- **GENERALIZED MARKET DEFINITION (based on readily
available figures requiring no special research)**

Present Size

 As Defined by Company's Trading Area

 As Defined by Growth Pattern in Area

 As Modified by Demographic Trends in Area

- **BRANDING REQUIREMENTS**

Appropriate Corporate Name Association

Existing Brand Fit

 Close-in Extender Potentials

 Affinity Flanker Potentials

 New Category Development Fit of Existing Brand

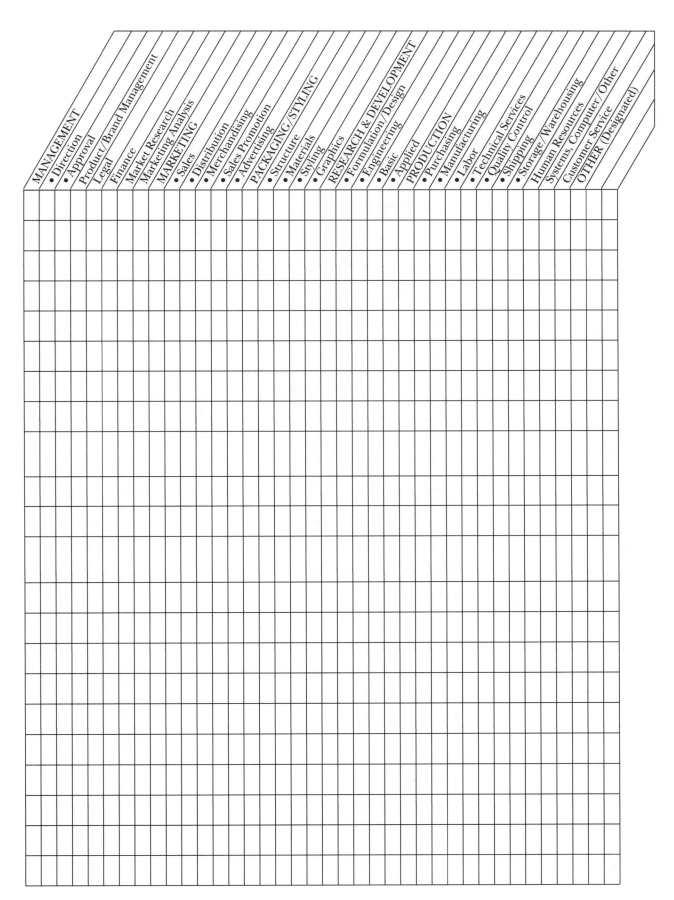

New Brand Required
Long-Term Expansion Predictability
New Generic Descriptor Required
Prospect/Customer/User Education
▪ **INNOVATION REQUIREMENTS**
Utilizes Existing Company Technology
Utilizes Known, Same or Related Industry Technology
Requires New APPLIED Science Technology
in Development
in Manufacturing
Invention Mode, Requires New, Basic Technology/Science
Review All of Above, as Basis for Business Analysis
▪ **BUSINESS ANALYSIS**
Company Has Needed Innovation Assets
Needs Refinement
Needs Specific Improvements
Dependable Life Forecast
Strategic Mission Sound
Needs Refinement
Needs Specific Improvement
Needs Redefinition
Needs Consideration of Alternatives/Substitute
Needs Review of Category Appropriateness

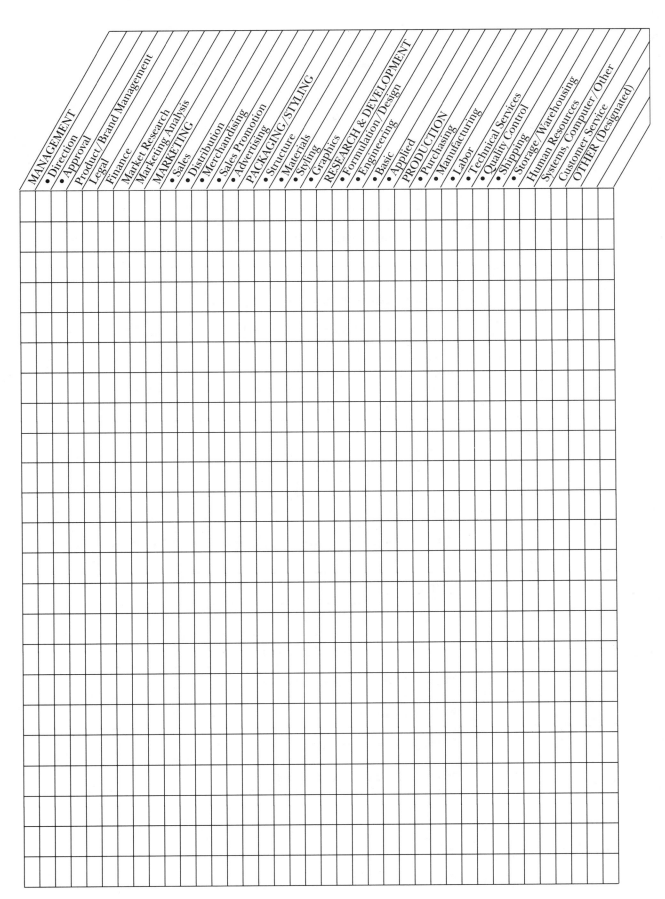

Preparation of Strategic Mission Statement

Assignment Responsibility*

Review/Input Sources

Approval Responsibility

Communication of Mission Statement to All Involved and Other Appropriate Parties

Publication of Mission Statement

Approval to Initiate:*

Program of Exploration

Opportunity Search and Identification (leading to . . .)

Specific New Product Objective

Management-Approved Plan to Activate Preliminary Conception and Investigation Steps—Detailed Opportunity Exploration

▪ **DECISION***

GO—Move on to next phase

GO—Extend/Enlarge/Embellish/Accelerate

GO—Modify, as Specified (time, budget, staff, etc.)

NO GO—Abort

NO GO—Pursue Substitute Opportunity

NO GO—Modify, as Specified

---

* Top management action/decision required

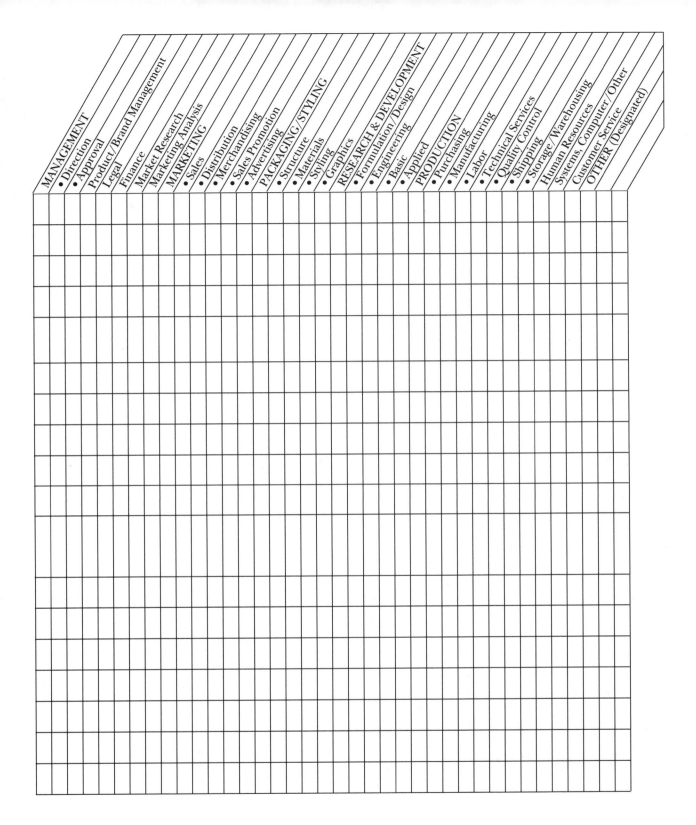

Exploration for Opportunity

Minimal investment thus far, except for normal staff, facilities and limited outside supplier resources.

Now the adventure begins.

The general definition of the goal has been set—but you need to draw a road map, select the right transportation and other logistics to successfully form a specific, detailed plan embodying articulated new product concepts for screening selection.

DEFINING THE SELECTED MARKET

That's the starting point. How alien or close it is to your present venue determines the degree of time and expense needed. In mass market categories, a great deal of needed information is public domain available from professional and trade resources, business publishers and sales audit services. Unfortunately, this is less true in emerging niche opportunities and in areas where product innovation may also require innovation in manufacturing and marketing channels.

It's too early to build a full-time team. It's not too early to identify critical players, to test possible later assignees and outside resources.

This checklist is a necessary start. Your answers to its category inquiries are a test of how far afield you need go in defining the market—before deciding on your invasion plans.

Industry Analysis

- **SALES VOLUME AND TRENDS**

  By Dollar Volume and Unit Sales

  By Specific Manufacturer/Marketer

  By Specific Product/Class

  By Geographic Region

  By Population Density

  By Economic Index (per capita consumption, buying power, etc.)

  By Media Efficiency (if applicable)

  By Customer Use Pattern (defined by frequency of purchase, use occasion)

  By Marketing Expenditure as percent of Sales, per Prospect Potential, etc.

- **BASIC TECHNOLOGY**

  State of the Art

  By Component Parts, Raw Materials, Labor Resources

  By Process, Assembly, Packaging, etc., Equipment and Subcontractor Resources

  By Patent Barriers, Opportunities

  By Purchasing

  By Transport

  By Storage

  Preliminary Verification of Technological Assumptions

  Technological Barriers Identified

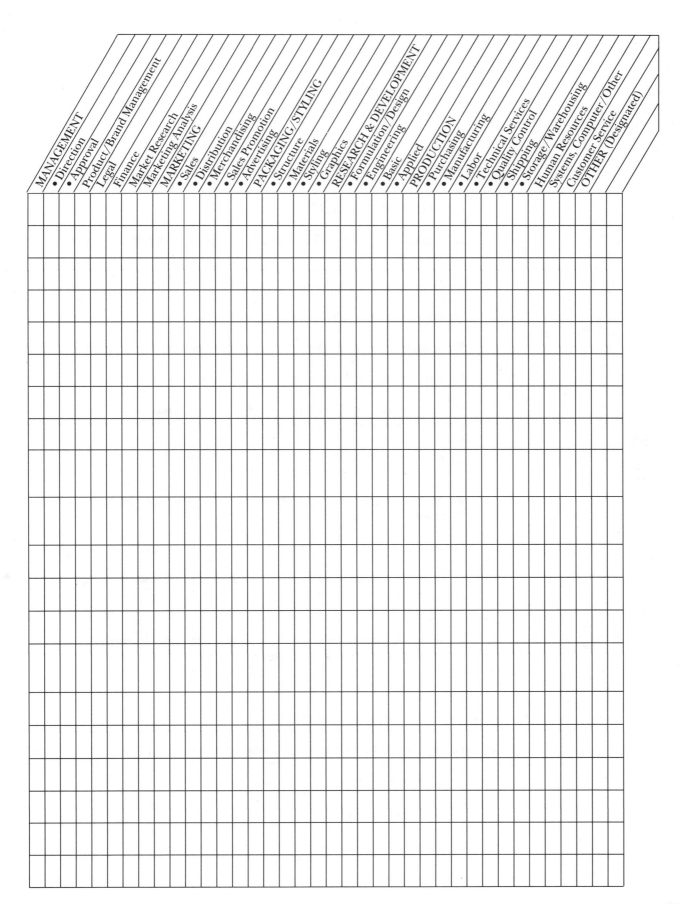

- **CUSTOMER DEFINITION**

  By Customer/Prospect Use Pattern (frequency of purchase, use occasion)

  By Demographic Characteristics

  By Psychographic Characteristics

  By Awareness of Category, Competitive Factors

  By Attitude toward Industry/Trade, Competitive Factors

  By Alternative and Substitute Products (are products first choices, brands first choices, is it an important decision, etc?)

  By Pricing Effects (inelastic, elastic, responsive to small, large, frequent, season, etc. price adjustments)

  By Regional and Seasonal Purchase, Use Patterns by Individual Products, Marketers

  Other Factors, as Available

    Outside Affecting Influences (foreign trade, regulatory restrictions, general consumption changes, ecological conditions, economic situation, etc.)

  Forecasts for the Industry and its Major Elements (growth, diversification, replacement, other changes)

- **DEFINITION OF SELECTED MARKET**

  Product Class Profile Study

  Survey of Product Class Components/Ingredients

    Design Standards

    General Technology

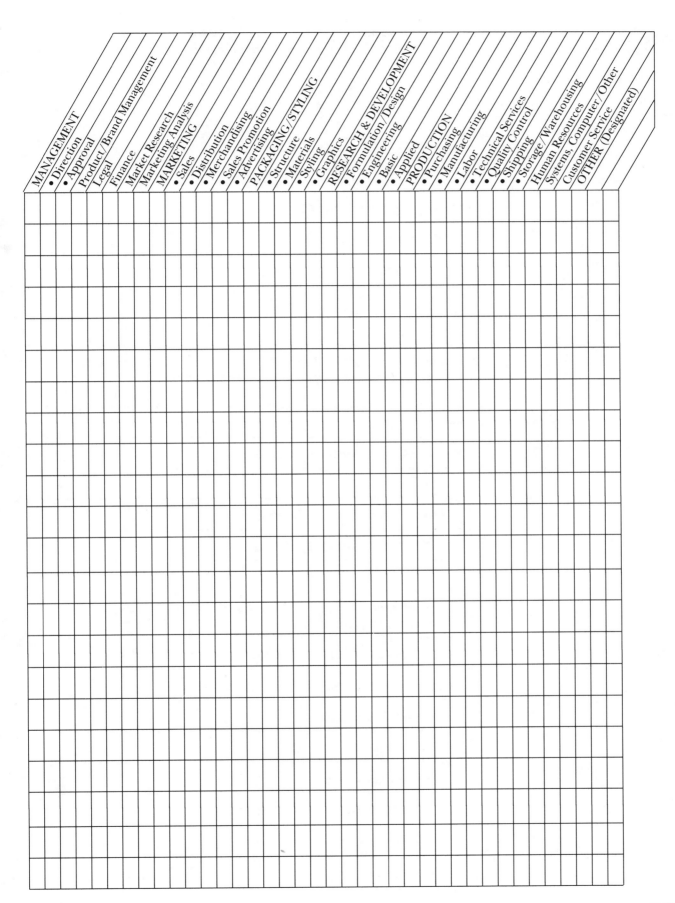

Survey of Selling Practices

Promotional Allowances

Selling Standards

Cyclical, Seasonal and Long-Term Marketing Considerations

Survey of Traditional Channels of:

Distribution

Other Channels of Distribution

Distribution Niche Opportunities

Survey of Trade Information (best available trade/industry/professional category data)

Cost of Goods Sold (@ Factory, estimate)

Direct Product Profitability (DPP) Summary

Wholesale Discounts

Promotional Allowances

Slotting Allowances

Minimum Trade Profit per Linear Foot

Distribution Costs

Shelf Management Costs

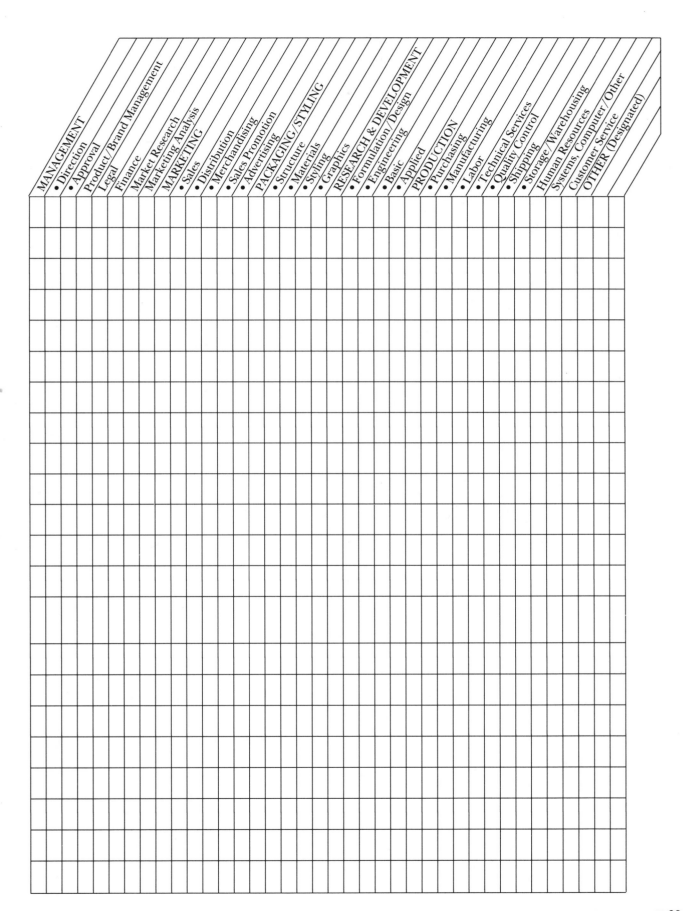

■ 33

Special Shipping/Added Costs

Special Stocking/Inventory Costs

Special Warehousing/Storage Costs

Point-of-Purchase Promotion Needs/Costs

Seasonal/Holiday Requirements

Survey of Regulations

Federal

State

Local (city, county, etc.)

International

Federal, State, Local and International Regulations in Reference to:

Ingredients

Raw Materials

Components

Label Restrictions

Ecology

Sizing

Package Form

Package Material

Selling/Pricing Practices

Other Controls:

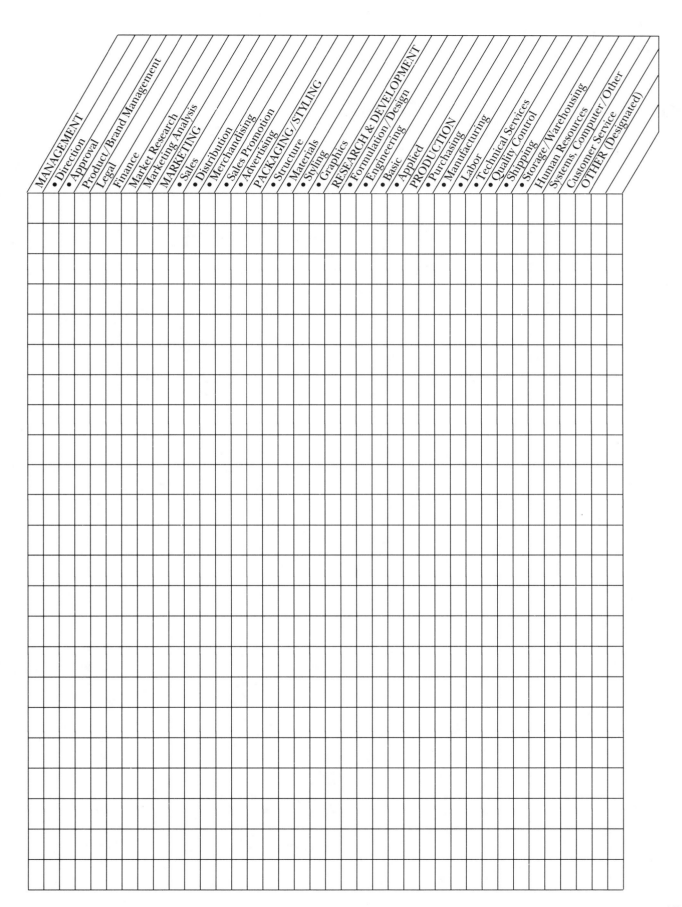

RESEARCHING THE COMPETITION

Whatever the product or service you are developing, there is always a *competitive set:* alternatives catering to the same customer needs as your offering. Even if you are pioneering a new, patented invention in an area never before addressed, you are still competing against alternative uses of time and money.

In most cases, you will likely be offering an alternative that will sell to an established market segment. It is, therefore, essential that your concept be superior in composition, performance, appearance, prestige, price, or accessibility.

For each new product or service you propose, you must know *all* about your competition. This is usually not a single competitor nor even one industry category. It can be a multi-variant set of competitors.

In major corporations, competitive intelligence is often the basis for a permanent department. Competition is so fierce, diverse, and specialized that research is a full-time activity. Although syndicated research services sell studies of all major categories, product, brand and company performance, there are special situations requiring customized research attention, specific to the company's targeted interests. Information must be regularly updated by internal resources, networks, and suppliers. The planned entry into a new field demands a new, focused research program. Don't overlook any information source. Often, department and trade associations in the new category can offer current information.

In setting up your competition research program, there are several bases to cover.

Look at the competitive products already on the market you plan to enter. Can your R&D and engineering departments brief you on technological advances and current practices in close-in fields? They should be assigned to keep track of any new related technologies. Follow up any networks or referrals they may have in allied fields. Test out relevant competitive products. Discover their strengths and flaws. Consider how your product will compete. This is standard operational practice.

Attend trade shows to see what competition is offering. Evaluate samples to find out how each competing product is put together and is packaged. Evaluate its marketing effectiveness. Analyze results of your market research. Determine if there are supplemental services which can dig deeper into the activities of your competitors.

Checklist 2.2 helps address these questions and others. It is a list of all aspects to consider before developing any new product for a competitive market. It will not only help find out who your competitors are and what they are currently marketing, but will help predict what new products each is likely to introduce before your new entry becomes established.

The checklist begins by requiring a product-by-product profile of each competitor. Use this section to help assess the performance claims and actual strengths and weaknesses of competitive offerings. This includes investigation of component suppliers to competition, often an indicated vulnerability.

Next, look at how your competitors market. The checklist provides a complete breakdown of the media use, the audiences reached and the investment efficiency of the media buys.

Look, too, at competitive selling themes, claims and the images projected by the advertising/promotion/merchandising executions. This will help identify opportunities for unique, new claims your product can be designed to deliver—as well as a distinctive, new image which will make the new product stand out.

The section of the checklist headed *Marketing Expenditure Analysis* helps provide a detailed review of competitive spending in each area of marketing. This will help in shaping the introductory plan to leverage the most initial acceptance and long-term most profitable sales volume.

The financial resources and stability of each competitor are important also. Study the investment trends of competition: how much they spend on new product development—and on competitive acquisitions and mergers. Do major competitors have the critical mass to accelerate the cost of your introduction, and to erect trade barriers? Or is your innovation so special that it fills a niche inappropriate to the identified giant competitors?

Finally, use the checklist to examine advantages your competitors have that will be difficult for you to match. Consider patents and other protections that may restrict your plans. To what extent does a competitor's success depend on a formula or production secret that you will not be able to uncover or imitate? Are there any other factors that will limit your entry into this market?

Only through a complete and thorough survey of the competition will you be able to narrow the field and discover where the best openings into a particular market lie. The checklist covers point by point each area of research on which you will need to work. Use it—as you used the Industry Analysis checklist—to assign responsibilities for examining and monitoring the competition to relevant departments within your organization. Set up the checklist at the outset of any new product development program and refer back to it at regular intervals throughout.

Competitive Set

- **PRODUCT-BY-PRODUCT COMPETITIVE PROFILE ANALYSIS**

In General:

Assets

Liabilities

Performance

Performance Claims

In Specifics:

By Trade Practices

By Product Specifications

By Product Reliability (including warranty practices, service, reputation)

By (relative/share) Product Sales Volume and Trends, as broken out from evaluations, estimates and projections from Sales Volume and Trends section)

By Advertising/Promotion Spending

- **ANALYSIS OF COMPETITIVE MEDIA USE**

Type (TV, radio, newspapers, magazines, billboards, mail, etc.)

Weight (impressions, coverage, frequency, size, etc.)

Seasonal

Time of Day

Day of Week

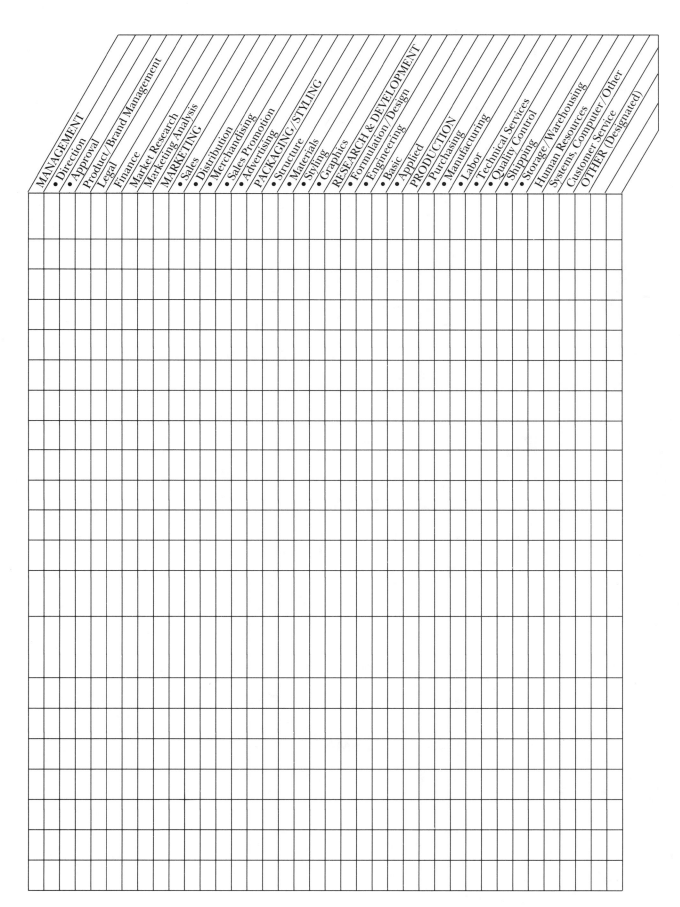

MANAGEMENT
• Direction
• Approval
Product/Brand Management
Legal
Finance
Market Research
Marketing Analysis
MARKETING
• Sales
• Distribution
• Merchandising
• Sales Promotion
• Advertising
PACKAGING/STYLING
• Structure
• Materials
• Styling
• Graphics
RESEARCH & DEVELOPMENT
• Formulation/Design
• Engineering
• Basic
• Applied
PRODUCTION
• Purchasing
• Manufacturing
• Labor
• Technical Services
• Quality Control
• Shipping
• Storage/Warehousing
Human Resources
Systems, Computer/Other
Customer Service
OTHER (Designated)

Holiday Considerations

Share of Product Category Media

Programming Adjacencies/Sponsorships

Geographic Coverage

Demographic Target(s), Users

Psychographic Target(s), Users

Spending/Budget Against Above Targets

- **SELLING THEMES**

Major Claims

Image Projected

- **MARKETING EXPENDITURE ANALYSIS**

By Marketing Spending Share Trends

By End-User and by Trade Channel Expenditure Ratios

By Sales Efficiency Related to Industry Averages, Leading Competitors and Trendlines

Analysis of Other Marketing Spending

Sales Force

Brokers

Distributors

Detailing

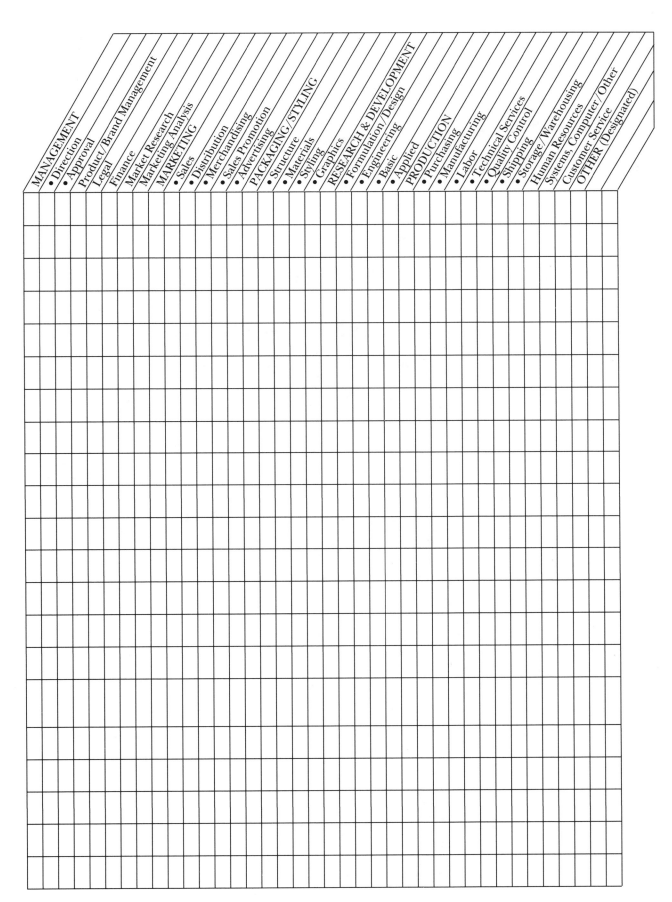

Sales Promotion

Relating to Category Share

Relating to Cost of Goods Sold

Analysis of Competitive Product/Brand History

Reasons: Actual (if known)

Reasons: Supposed

Competitive Reaction Tactics Employed

- **ANALYSIS OF COMPETITIVE SUPPLIER RESOURCES**

Raw Materials

Research & Development/Engineering

Manufacturing

Packaging

- **ANALYSIS OF COMPETITIVE FINANCIAL MANAGEMENT/ RESOURCES**

Near Term

Long Term

Innovation Investment History

Management Stability

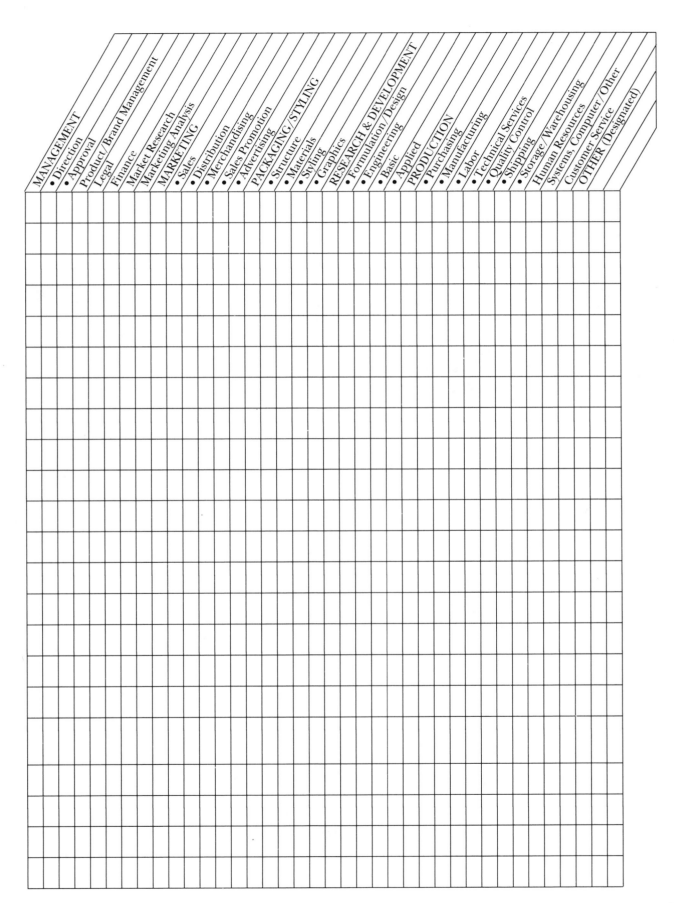

Diversionary Issues

- **ANALYSIS OF DIFFICULT-TO-PREEMPT ADVANTAGES**

Patents

Trademarks

Copyrights

Trade &/or Formula &/or Production Secrets

Captive Suppliers

Captive Outlets

Critical Mass

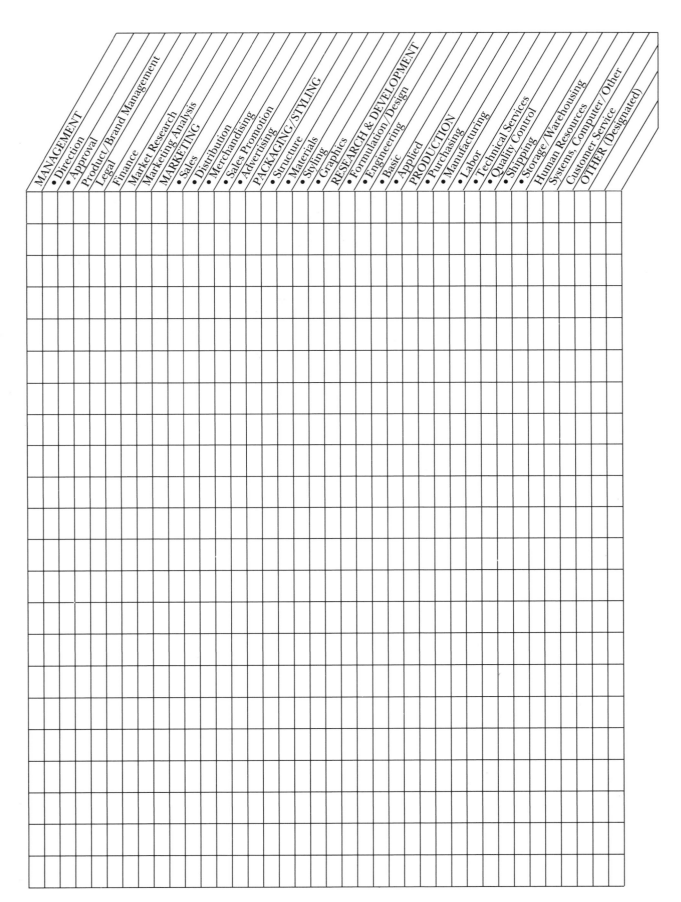

OPPORTUNITY DEFINITION

Working through this checklist helps define the extent of the challenge—and the possible reward. It also puts dimensions on amounts at risk in time, money and human resources.

If the net effect of delivery on the opportunity looks meager, then it should be back to the beginning of the process, in order to best leverage your strengths. Proper deployment behind new product developments which may lead to line scope and longevity is essential.

The object of this phase of the process is to refine the *Concept Focus Area.* To do this sufficiently well may require a preliminary survey of prospect interest in the end-user deliveries. If this looks sufficiently promising, then it justifies the commitment the new product objective will entail, including the ensuing refined exploratory and creative conceptual activities and (possibly) redirected company resources.

You are about to unleash flights of fantasy—albeit in a controlled atmosphere!

■ CHECKLIST 2.3

Opportunity Definition

Opportunity Definition

- **PRODUCT OPPORTUNITY**

  New to Marketplace

  New to Category

  New Category for Company

  New to Existing Company Category

  New to Company Brand

    Line Extension

    Flanker

  New Brand

- **PRODUCT ROLE**

  Maintenance

  Defensive

  Future Foothold

  Preempt Anticipated Competition

  Broaden Business Base

  Leverage New Expertise/Invention/Resources

- **PRODUCT LEVERAGE**

  Capacity

  Excess/Off-Season/Location

  Technology

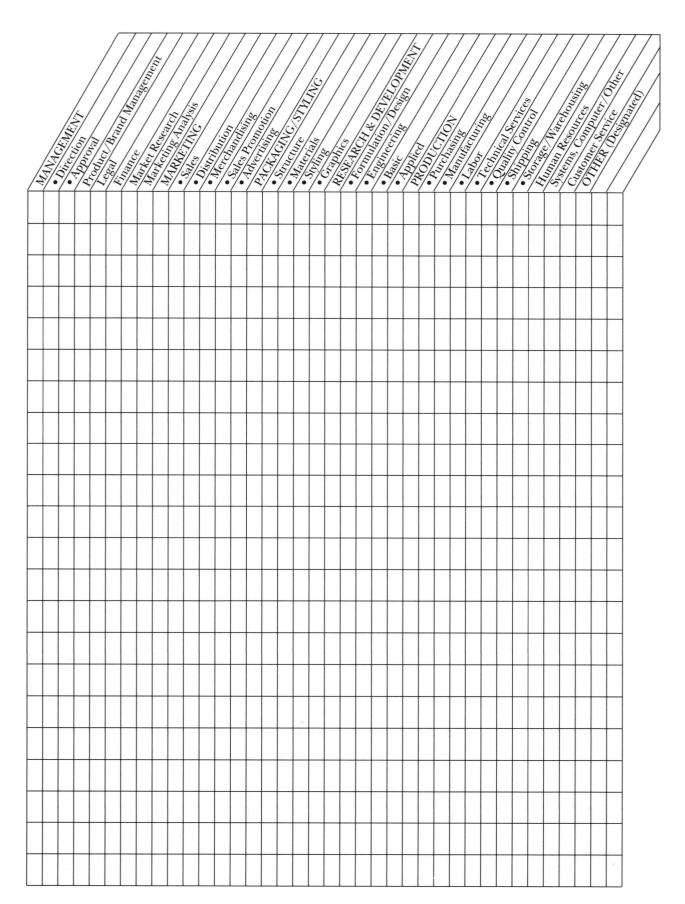

Distribution

Exclusive License

- **OTHER BENEFITS TO COMPANY**

Cost Reduction

Repositioning in/out of Category/Brand

Product Revisions/Improvements

- **OTHER PARAMETERS/CONSIDERATIONS**

Safety

Environmental Standards

Quality Assurance

Reliability/Servicing Required

Maintainability/Servicing Required

Performance Requirements

- **SURVEY OF POTENTIAL END-USER INTEREST IN CONCEPT FOCUS AREA**

- **SURVEY FINDINGS REPORT**

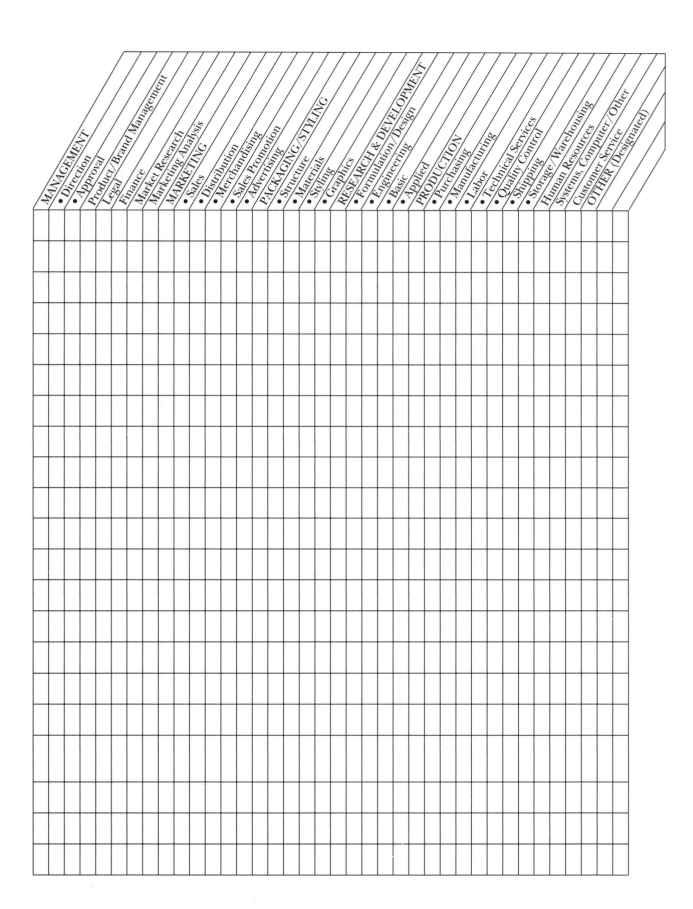

SPECIFIC NEW PRODUCT OBJECTIVE— CREATIVITY COMMENCES

With all the input at hand from the earlier phases of the process, idea exploration and conceptual activities begin.

Staffing is key. There are no formal rules. Everyone should be encouraged to work in his or her way, individually, off campus, in teams, in group retreats, involving confidentiality-cleared outsiders, regularly contracted ones and special project appointees: specialists, gurus, enablers, off-the-wall stimulators, graphic visualizers, articulate dreamers—dial-in special purpose as well as gestalt assistance. The management-designated leader should have (budgeted) free rein to make this phase in-house culture-busting and synergy enhancing. You want to see both the forest and the trees—and what is hidden within it and behind them.

Best filter for the inspirations is each champion's articulation of the concept in as concrete a form as is practicable at this early stage—to show performance and appearance, for starters. Big budget working prototypes are for later, when the specific product objective is approved.

PRE-DEVELOPMENT ANALYSIS

Now you have narrowed your Concept Focus area and are ready to outline your plans in specific terms. The next checklist is used to explore the range of tasks and to assign responsibilities for getting the ideas shaped into reality.

Look at Checklist 2.4, *Pre-Development Analysis.* The first stage is to examine the feasibility of each new idea. One measure is a rough forecast of sales in defined markets, including potential market share. Necessary investment and risk estimates are made. Very helpful at this point are war game exercises. They can help simulate competitive and industry environments to be entered, and will help determine how well the new product will be accepted.

In the second section, *Creative Conceptual Activities,* the checklist outlines specific new product creative work areas. Everyone involved is encouraged to submit ideas, working in any style—whether individually, in pairs, in teams, in group retreats, on or off campus—whatever is most productive. Frequently helpful, at this juncture, is input from outside specialists and consultants. With so many involved, the checklist helps keep track. It can also list any special venture groups, task forces, or agencies working on specific creative projects.

The checklist helps define exactly the creative tasks the new concept requires. Is it an innovation or an invention? Is it a product replacement or modification? And to what extent will it require new technology in development and/or manufacture?

Next, the checklist provides for a detailed description of the new product with applicable formulas, recipes, designs or, in critical cases, a prototype working model. Check off specific requirements and assign responsibilities.

Finally, the checklist supplies a rough guide in preparing a preliminary estimate of the cost of developing the product, in terms of staff, equipment, supplies, and outside resources.

The information gathered will be used in the product approval process. Be certain it is thorough, detailed and exact as possible, to facilitate the necessary decisions.

Pre-development Analysis

- **FEASIBILITY ANALYSIS**

Define Target Markets

Forecast Sales Volume and Potential Market Share

Perform a Risk-ratio Analysis

Conduct a Preliminary Feasibility Study

Using Secondary Data (not prototypes or trial runs)

Using Expert Professional Opinion

Use Testing Techniques or War Game Exercises to:

Assess Competitive Reaction

Assess Exclusivity

Assess Regulatory Constraints or Protection

Examine any Exceptional Technical Hurdles

Consider Legal and Policy Issues

- **CREATIVE CONCEPTUAL ACTIVITIES**

Departmental

Venture Groups®

Task Forces

Staff Individuals

Retained Outside Resources

Presently Contracted, i.e. Advertising Agency, Professional and Technical Specialists, etc.

® Venture Group is registered Service Trademark, U.S. Patent Office No. 920358

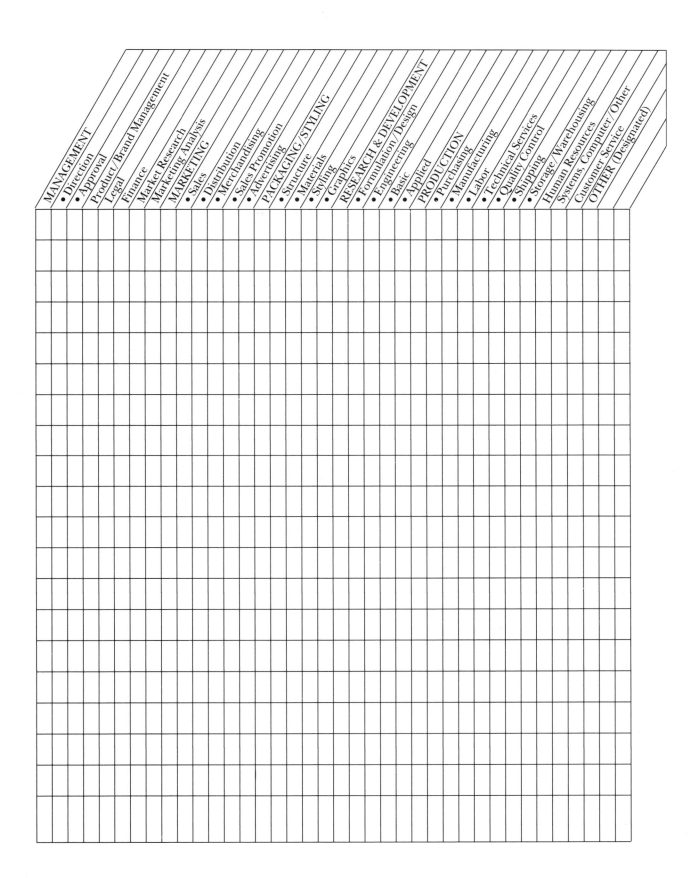

Specially Contracted, i.e. Consultants, Laboratories, etc.

Define Broad Concept Direction Tasks

Replace

Improve

Innovate

Invent

Explore/Discover

Pioneer

Applied Technology

Evolve Basic Science

- **SUMMARY OF PRODUCT IDEA(S)**

Statement (Description)

Diagram/Illustration (if applicable)

Appearance

Function/Performance

Results

Example

Affinity Products/Services

Rough Prototype(s), Non-Functional

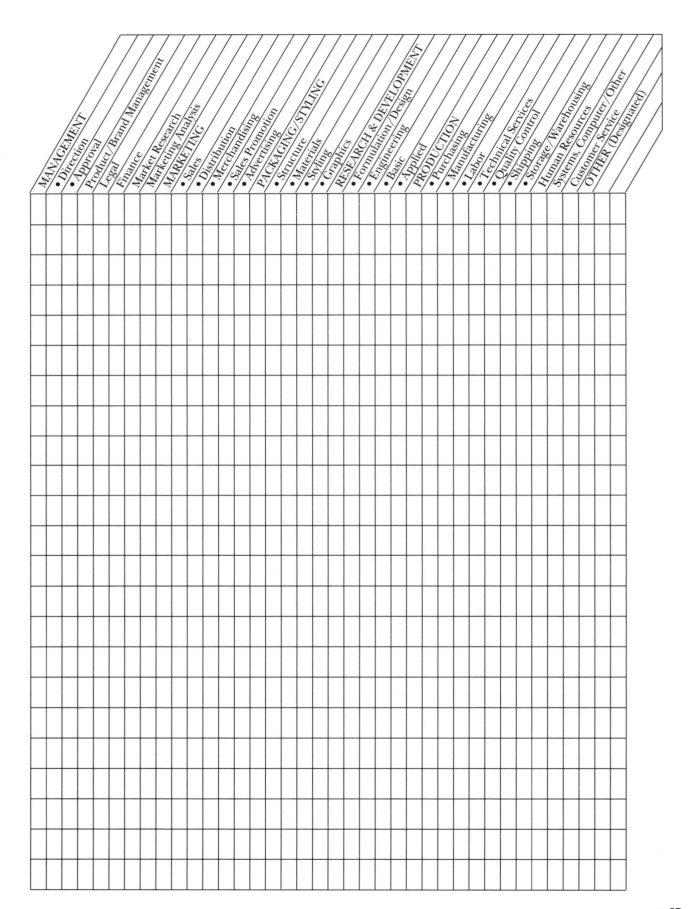

Rough Working Model(s)

Other:

- **EVALUATION OF MERIT**

- **PRELIMINARY OPPORTUNITY ESTIMATE(S), FROM INCEPTION THROUGH SUBSEQUENT STEPS, INCLUDING:**

  Commercialization Costs

  Lifespan Cost

  Lifespan Yield

  Break-Even Point

  Other:

- **TIGHT COST ESTIMATE FOR NEXT PHASE ONLY**

  Staff Time

  Supplies and Equipment

  Outside Resources

  Related Expenses

- **APPROVED***

  Plan and Budget to Investigate (Screening)

---

* Top management action/decision required

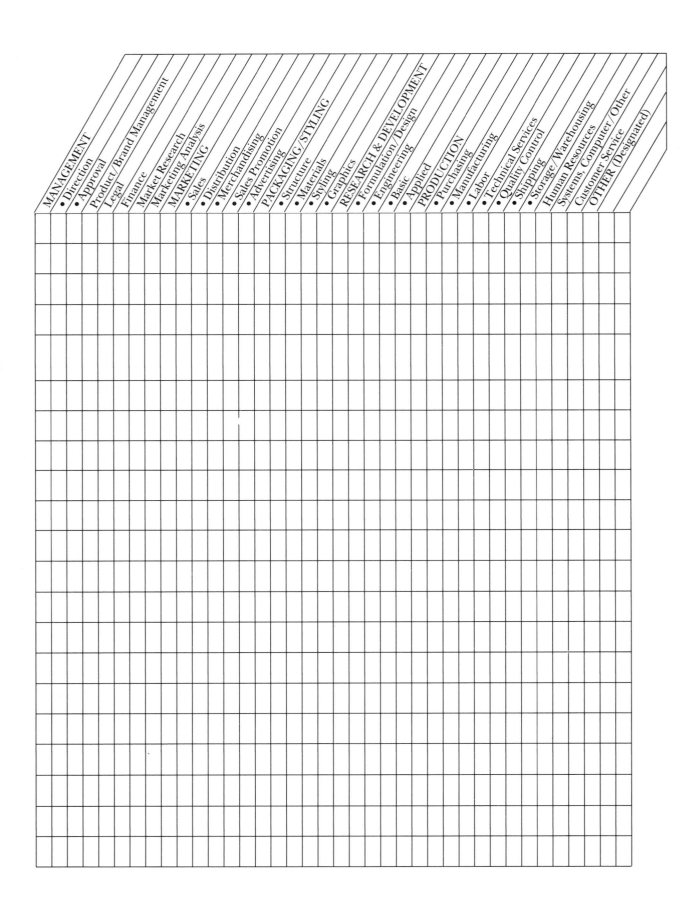

- **DECISION***

  GO—Move on to next phase

  GO—Extend/Enlarge/Embellish/Accelerate

  GO—Modify, as Specified (time, budget, staff, etc.)

  NO GO—Abort

  NO GO—Pursue Substitute Opportunity

  NO GO—Modify, as Specified

---

* Top management action/decision required

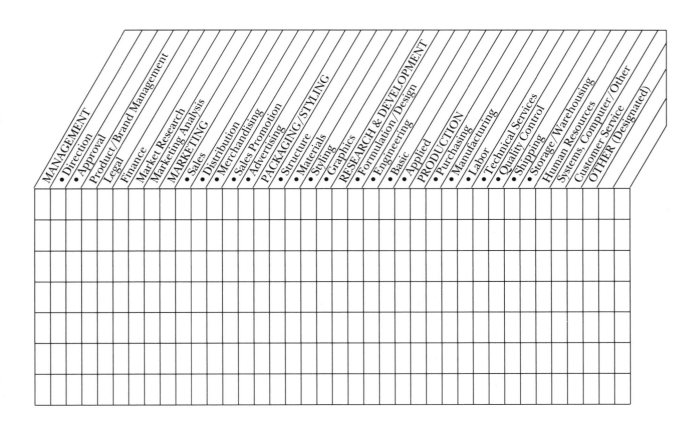

Screening New Ideas

By this stage, the checklist system has helped identify areas of new product development in which you have the unique expertise, resources, marketing awareness, and customer base necessary to succeed. There are many new ideas which fall loosely within the Concept Focus Area. Wide-ranging research has stimulated enthusiasm and involvement among staff, suppliers, and outside consultants. Top management has given the go ahead to isolate and follow up the most promising opportunities. Look carefully at each of the players, and pick the potential champions, and focus attention and resources on them. Not every new idea will cross the finish line—many will fall at the first hurdle. That first hurdle is the screening process.

SELECTING THE WINNERS

The screening process gets down to specifics. Evaluate each new idea, objectively, on its own merits. Every suggestion, every criticism, every problem, every imaginable opportunity and objection must be probed, analyzed, estimated, and reported. Nothing should be overlooked. All parties to the program should participate, and all judgments should be evaluated. Imagine you are an attorney preparing for a jury trial. You anticipate as much as possible, gathering together the facts needed before entering the courtroom. You prepare persuasive arguments and exhibits, and you back them up with hard evidence if you are going to win your case.

The ideas to be screened will vary in many ways: in the investment required for their development, production technology, components and equipment, as well as the various styling, packaging, trade names, features and positionings to be marketed via the most appropriate sales and distribution channels. The project team must organize and screen all these variables so that the product idea can be presented in a workable and affordable format.

The best way to screen ideas is to determine how well they are likely to perform against influences prevailing in the organization and in the marketplace. Gather specific information or accurate estimates of exactly what will be involved in each stage of the proposed product development process, from manufacture, through initial marketing, to long-term sales and distribution.

The appointed Project Coordinating Executive will, in most instances, screen the marketplace opportunities first. Usually, this requires the least expense and the analysis can either help justify the heavier expense involved in other departmental projects—or, if the market potential does not appear attractive, save this investment for more promising future projects.

Nevertheless, each potentially affected department should be given an opportunity to input facts and speculations in the early phases, where astute judgment is critically important.

The five key areas to be considered are delineated in the checklist, which is designed to help make sure each area is adequately covered. Each department is encouraged to add to it, modify it, and tailor it to the requirements of each new idea, according to each perception of its development.

■ CHECKLIST 3.1

Screening New Ideas

- **APPOINT PROJECT COORDINATOR***

- **PRODUCT SPECIFICATIONS**

  Define the Specific Form the Product is Likely to Take

  Analyze Sizes, Colors, Shapes, Textures, Types to Be Developed

  Finalize Suggested Prototype

  Prepare Dummy Prototype, Complete with Packaging, Labeling, etc.

  Prepare Visual Representation and Supporting Descriptors

  Analyze Human and Other Resource Requirements

- **MAINTENANCE/SERVICING REQUIREMENTS**

  Analyze After-sales Maintenance or Servicing Product Will Require

  Analyze Warranty/Guarantee Needs

  Examine Effect on Existing Product Insurance or Product Liability Arrangements

- **MARKETING SPECIFICATIONS**

  Research User Satisfaction with Current Products in Category

  Prepare Marketing/Promotion/Advertising Exhibits

  Select Potential Marketing/Brand Claims

  Test How Well Claims Are Likely to Motivate Users

  Decide How Price Will Be Fixed

---

* Top management action/decision required

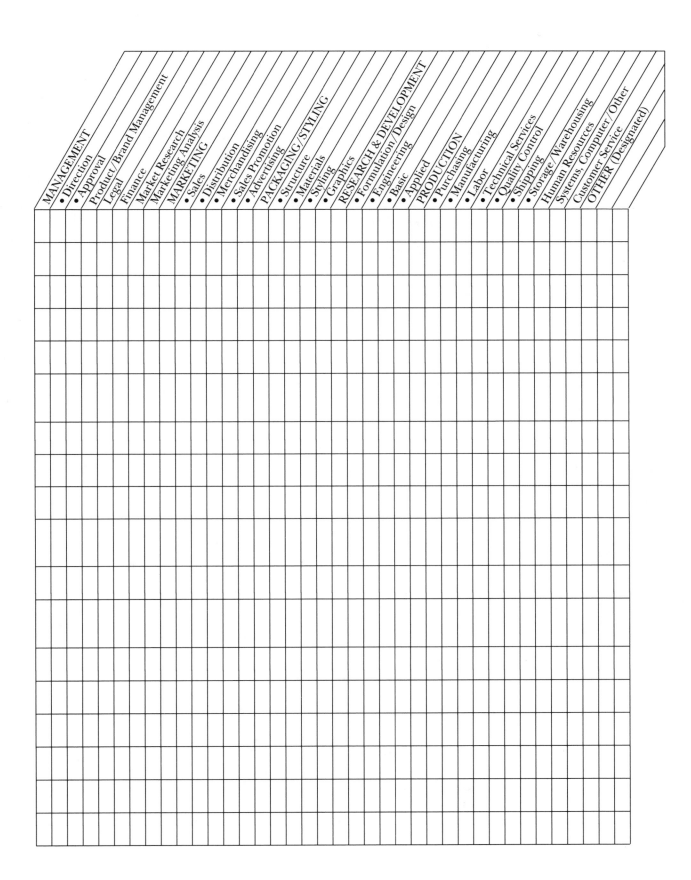

- **SALES/DISTRIBUTION**

  Estimate Projected Income from Selected Target Markets

  Estimate Projected Income from Secondary or Adjunct Markets

  Government

  Institutions

  Private Labels

  Special Licensing

  Premiums

  Export

  Special Foreign Products, Services, Brands

  Foreign Manufactured for Foreign Sales

  Foreign Manufactured for Import Sales

  Domestic Manufactured for Export Sales

- **LONG-TERM ATTRIBUTES**

  Estimate Period of Product Exclusivity

  Estimate Time Frame for Significant Upgrades, Improvements, Innovations of Base Product

  Estimate of Replacement of Current Products as Opportunity per User, per Percentage of Use per User

  Estimate Additional Users Brought into Category by New Product

- **REPORT FINDINGS AND INDICATED OPPORTUNITIES**

- **AUTHORIZATION TO SUBMIT FORMAL BUDGET, STAFF PROPOSAL***

---

* Top management action/decision required

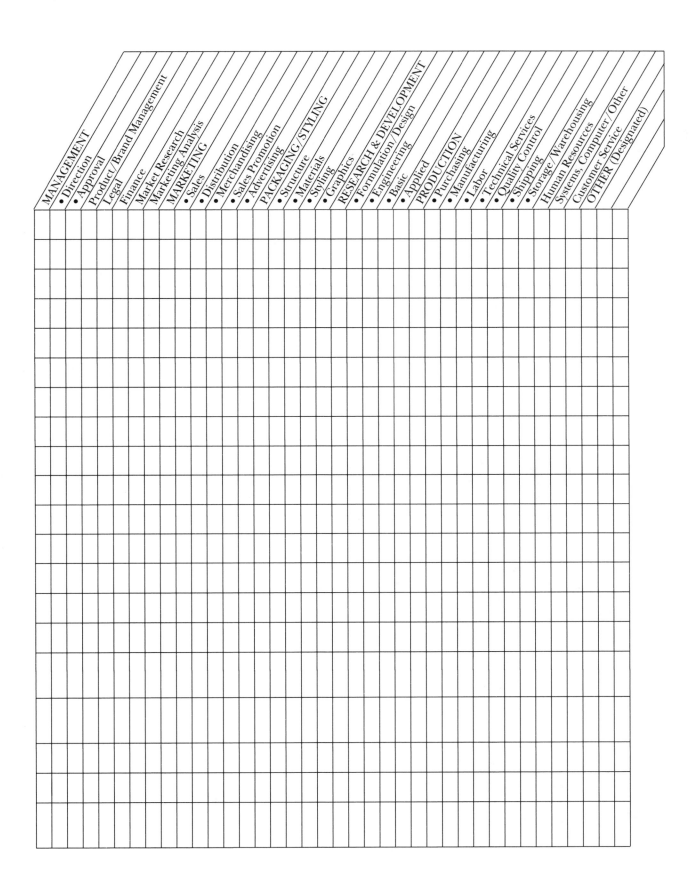

- **DECISION***

GO—Move on to Next Phase

GO—Extend/Enlarge/Embellish/Accelerate

GO—Modify, as Specified (time, budget, staff, etc.)

NO GO—Abort

NO GO—Pursue Substitute Opportunity

NO GO—Modify, as Specified

* Top management action/decision required

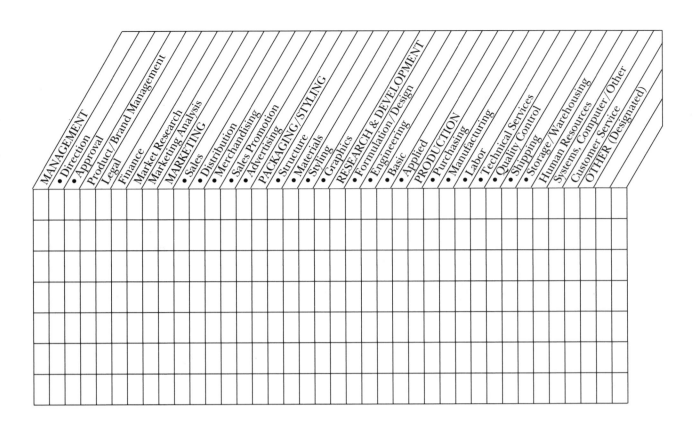

Making a Proposal

The proposal stage is the last phase of pre-development approval. This is where details of the new product introduction—particularly financial details—are finalized. Major investment decisions are made on this basis. It is essential to present well-informed, accurate data to management. The highest level of expertise is essential, with all involved in the project consulted.

Management will pay close attention during the proposal stage. Expenditure is increasing, and future investment levels are being set. Any errors or miscalculations can jeopardize the whole enterprise.

GETTING SPECIFIC

Checklist 4.1 helps maximize the relevance and accuracy of the information in the new product proposal. It lists data needed for the new product project's approval: financial, legal, manufacturing, and marketing.

Most importantly—the proposal should provide a detailed forecast of predicted expenditure. This will include research & development and manufacturing budgets. The initial cost estimates should be based on optimal manufacturing levels, with start-up costs listed separately. Other financial considerations might result from staffing changes; changes in local tax payments due to operational changes; or hiring of special, additional start-up services. Use the checklist to allocate responsibilities for providing accurate cost estimates, and for keeping track of expenditure throughout the development process.

Next, consider any legal aspects that need to be finalized before new product introduction.

The checklist also summarizes the key manufacturing elements to be involved, from formulation of designs, through testing of component parts and prototypes, to technical feasibility tests.

Lastly, marketing considerations are listed, many based largely on earlier market research. Now, the information your staff, consultants, and suppliers provide must be much more detailed to aid in making specific forecasts of potential sales and profitability levels. You also need data on the specific market segments targeted by your new products. Include plans to carry out evaluative tests on the new product with perspective buyers.

Use the checklist as a blueprint for preparing the new product proposal you will present to management for approval. Make sure you modify it to suit the needs of the industry category, the market, and your organization. Anticipate *all* organizational or operational changes that will be required to make your new product or service a success. By circulating the checklist to as wide a panel of staff and outside advisors as possible, you can create an accurate picture of how the new product will fit in: how it will affect current operations, and how it will benefit the organization. At later stages of the development process, you will need to check back with the approved proposal to make sure everything is going as planned. A comprehensive checklist makes it much easier to measure progress, and ensure continuing approval from management.

Preparing a Proposal

- **AUTHORIZATION OF PLANNED DEVELOPMENT PROGRAM, WITH ESTIMATED INVESTMENT AND TIMETABLE***

- **APPROVAL OF FIRST PHASE RESEARCH & DEVELOPMENT/ENGINEERING BUDGET***

- **FINANCIAL DATA**

- **Initial Cost Estimates (based on optimal manufacturing levels)**

- **Additional Start-up Cost Estimates**

- **Other Financial Considerations**

    Changes in Staff Levels

    Local Taxes Payable

    Temporary Start-up Services

- **LEGAL DATA**

    Government Clearance/Approval Plans

    Applications Filing Plans

    Copyrights

    Trademarks

    Patents

    Licensing

* Top management action/decision required

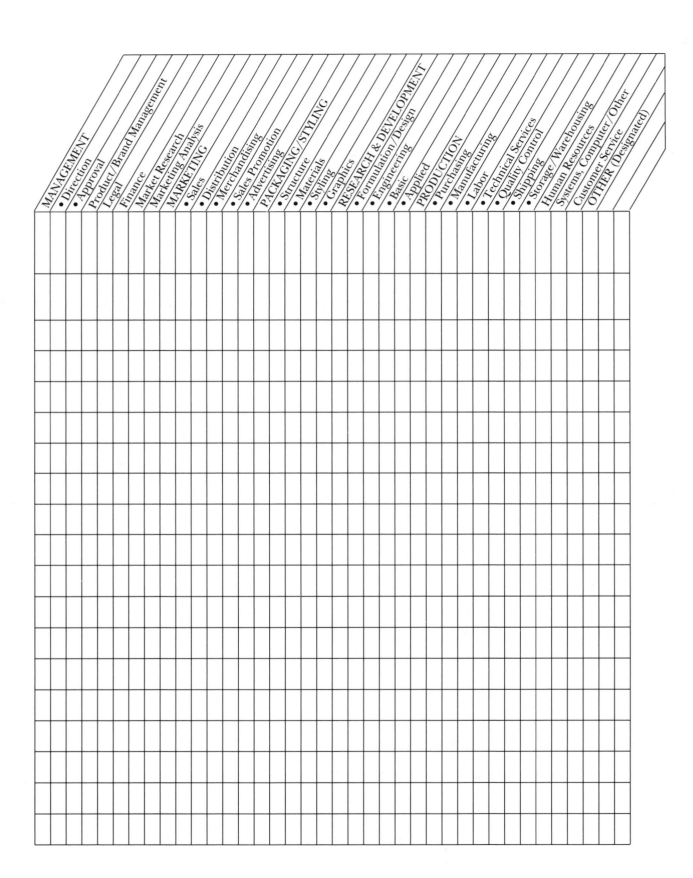

- **MANUFACTURING DATA**

Facilities Requirements

    Capacity

    Availability

    Subcontracting Plan

Design

    Specifications/Renderings

    Models/Working Prototypes

    Estimate of Performance Potential

    Life and Fatigue Test of Materials, Finishes, etc.

    Independent Laboratory/Engineering Analysis of Prototypes*

    Performance and Efficiency Test

    Technical Feasibility of Manufacturing

- **MARKETING DATA**

Product Platform Preparation

Communications Creative Blueprint

Evaluation of Present Users and New Product Prospects in Market Target Segment

Market Profile and Near-term Sales Forecast

Price and Profit Structure (economic potential)

Evaluation of Prototype by Prospects

Competitive Comparison (e.g. blind and double blind tests)

---

* Top management action/decision required

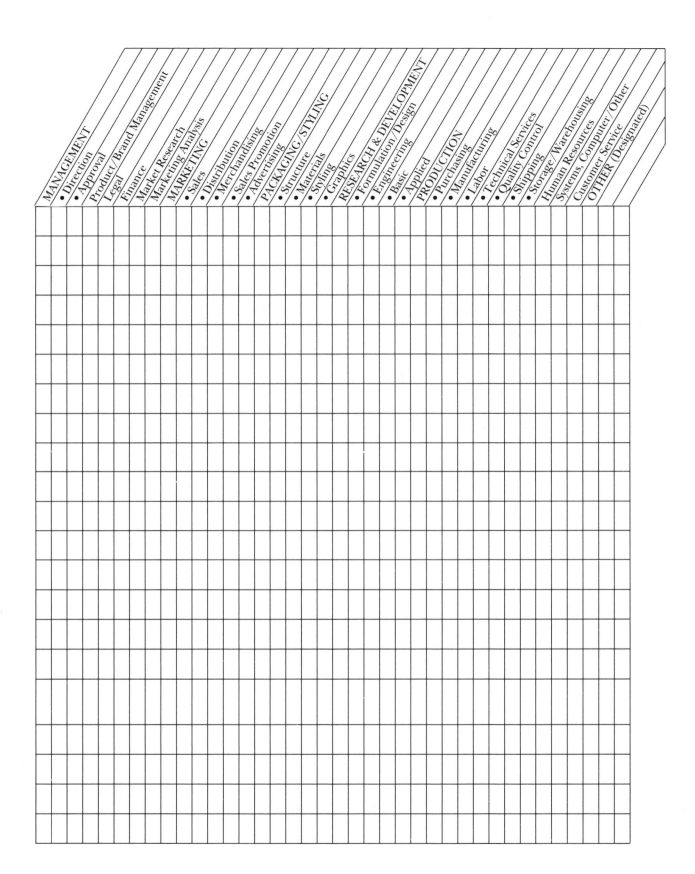

■ 75

Implementation of Potential (prospect needs-related)
Forecast of New Product Volume Potential
▪ **UPDATED BUDGET FORECAST**
▪ **REQUEST FOR PROPOSAL APPROVAL**
▪ **DECISION***
GO—Move on to Next Phase
GO—Extend/Enlarge/Embellish/Accelerate
GO—Modify, as Specified (time, budget, staff, etc.)
NO GO—Abort
NO GO—Pursue Substitute Opportunity
NO GO—Modify as Specified

---

* Top management action/decision required

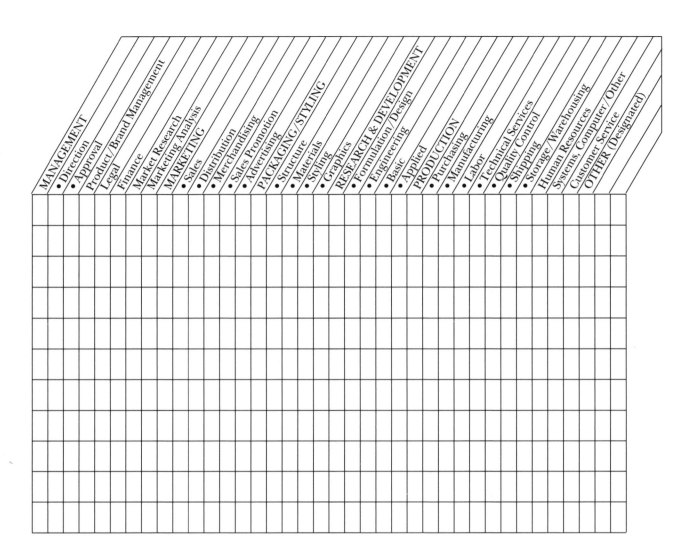

Development

The new product to be introduced has been approved on the basis of the feasibility and profitability forecasts. The project is becoming a reality, backed by investment and resources. It's time to approach the starting gate.

The next step is to develop the new product to meet the specificiations, time and cost budgets.

Checklist 5.1 is a management tool that helps coordinate and control the various interrelated processes of new product design, implementation, and testing. Every aspect of development, from manufacturing to testing prototypes, to packaging and labeling finished products, is listed here.

The development process is divided into four distinct sections on the checklist: prototypes, full-scale production, packaging and labeling, and market planning.

First, look at the production requirements for designing and manufacturing prototypes. The prototype will be used for testing product appearance, as well as performance, safety, and quality control—technological assumptions made during the earlier ideas stage.

Once successful prototypes have been developed, the next step is to identify resources, raw materials, and components needed for full-scale production. Confirm or modify earlier cost and time estimates.

Next, look at the packaging and labeling requirements of each variation or model of the new product. Coordinate the design and testing of packaging, brand name and product descriptor alternatives.

The last section of the checklist summarizes market planning to be carried out during the development stage. This includes various aspects of the media, promotion, and market testing programs planned for the new product launch.

Work through the checklist before going into production. Confirm participants' contributions and areas of responsibility. Refer to the checklist periodically to make sure everything is going according to plan.

The Development Stage

- **DEVELOP WORKING PROTOTYPES/MODELS**

  Large Scale Use-Research of Same

  To Assess Product/System/Process Performance Requirements for:

  Safety

  Environment

  Quality

  Reliability

  Maintainability

- **ESTABLISH PERFORMANCE REQUIREMENTS FOR ALL COMPONENTS**

- **IDENTIFY COST AND AVAILABILITY OF:**

  Raw Materials

  Processing Hardware

  Required Components

- **ESTIMATE MANUFACTURING COST AND CAPITAL INVESTMENT FOR EACH LEVEL OF PRODUCTION**

  Confirm Estimate via (one or more of following):

  Operational Test of Prototype System/Process

  Pilot Plant Test

  Full Scale Simulation

- **VERIFY ALL TECHNOLOGICAL ASSUMPTIONS**

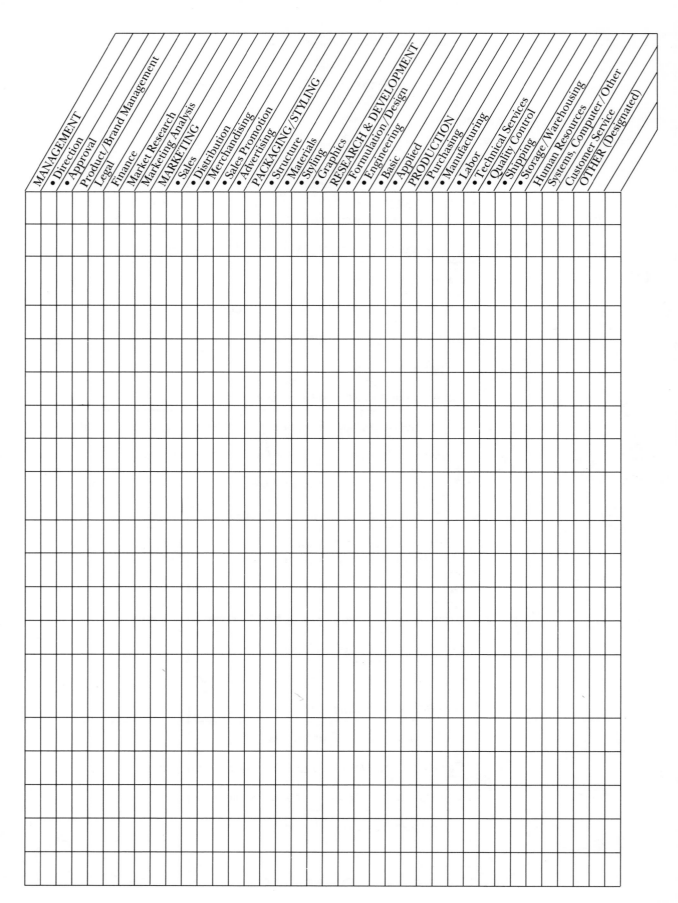

■ **COST ESTIMATE FOR FULL DEVELOPMENT STAGE***
  (Basis for Appropriation)

Procurement/Purchasing Materials/Components Plan

Labor Availability

Labor/Union Requirements/Regulations

Packaging Regulations (Safety, etc.)

Shipping Regulations

Plant Capacity and Facilities Availability

Plant Location(s) and intra/inter Plant Shipping Requirements

---

Lead-time Estimate to Market Quantity Production

Develop Full Expansion Area Media Plan

  (Local, Regional, National, International)

**Select (co/contracted) Manufacturer Association and its
Identification (if any) with/on Product**

Generate and Screen Brand Name Possibilities

Create New or Select Established Generic Descriptor(s)

Legal Search of Brand Name Candidates

Register Trademark, Copyright Brand Name

Develop Basic Selling Theme(s)

Outline Labeling Requirements

Construct and Design Initial Packaging Alternatives

Test Packaging Options for Use, Appearance

Approve Package (and Inserts)

---

* Top management action/decision required

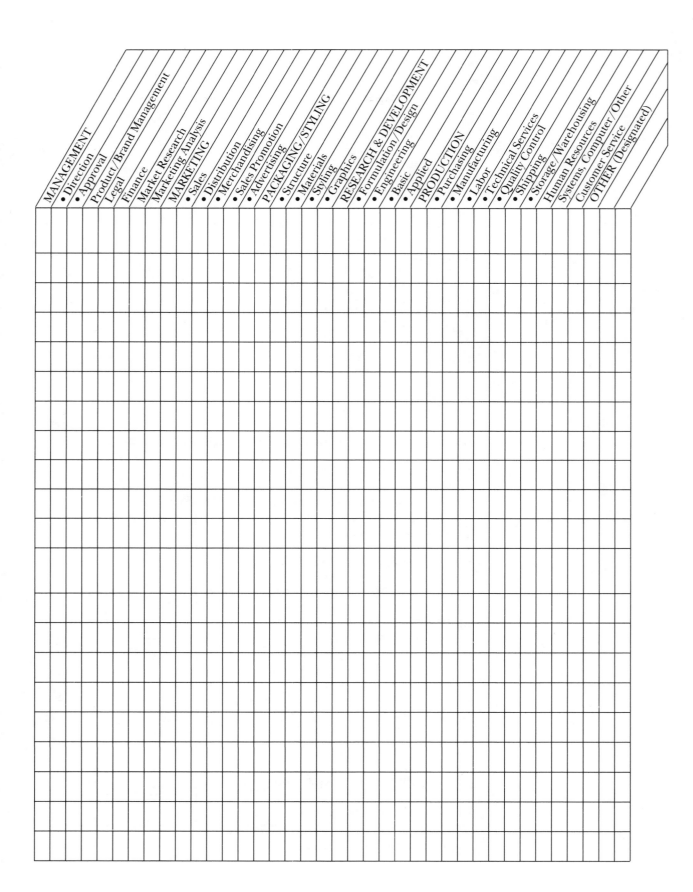

Prepare Directions/Contents Labeling to Conform

Adopt Media Guidelines, based on:

Selling Theme

Coverage of Prospects

Availability

Budget

Test Same, with Execution of Advertising Theme Presentation

Develop Total Communications Concept in Prototype Formats

Predict Competitive Reaction to New Product

Predict Competitive Reaction to Advertising/Promotion

Summarize ALL of Above

Updated Budget Forecast

▪ **REQUEST APPROVAL FOR NEXT PHASE**

▪ **DECISION***

GO—Move on to next phase

GO—Extend/Enlarge/Embellish/Accelerate

GO—Modify, as Specified (time, budget, staff, etc.)

NO GO—Abort

NO GO—Pursue Substitute Opportunity

NO GO—Modify, as Specified

---

* Top management action/decision required

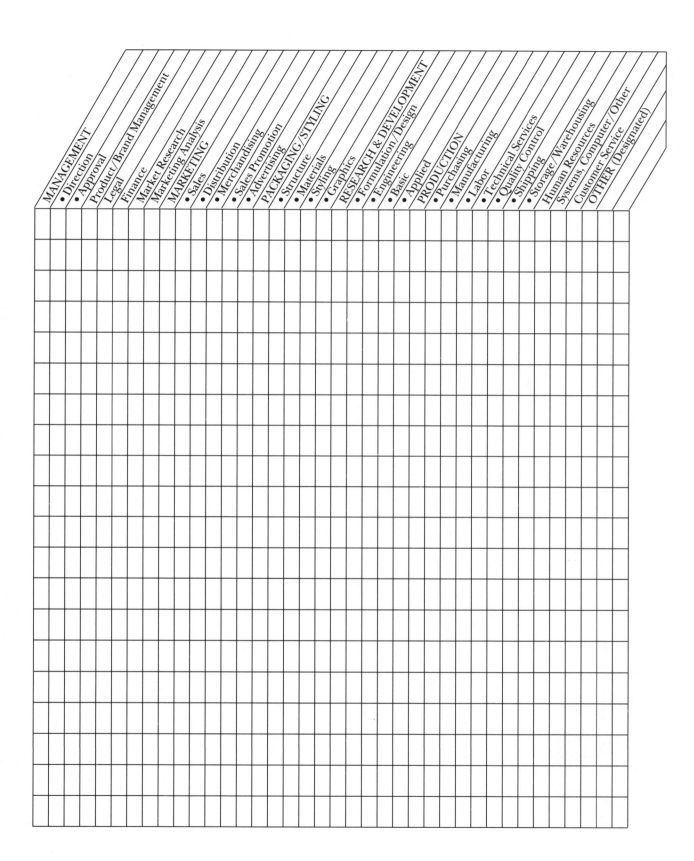

Market Testing

The purpose of test marketing is to simulate in a test environment conditions of a later, full-scale market launch. It is often through test markets that many new products are born into real market conditions. They will be evaluated in terms of quality and performance by trade prospects, users, and by competition.

Make sure that the test market is fully representative of the intended expansion area. When choosing a geographic region to test, don't select the area in which you currently have either your strongest or weakest customer base. Choose an area where you have an average level of sales. If the entry is your first in the category, then select an average sales area for the category. Also, don't pick an area used often by other companies for market testing. Customer patterns here are unlikely to be typical, and therefore not indicative of expansion area market conditions.

DEVISING A TESTING PROGRAM

Checklist 6.1 summarizes the elements that should be considered in a comprehensive market testing program.

First, define clear and realistic sales objectives for the test markets. Decide the minimum level of sales necessary within a defined time frame to make the market test a success.

Next, choose the test markets. Carry out analyses of each area under consideration and finalize selection.

Having identified test markets, begin promotional, advertising, and media planning. The checklist specifies all aspects to consider before launching any new product into the test area. At this stage, anticipate competitive reaction to the new product and set up counter-offensive plans.

Next, devise measures for evaluating the new product's performance in the test areas. Did it meet projected sales volume within the time frame prescribed? Did it meet acceptable levels of customer satisfaction?

Depending on the results of test marketing, the final step is to decide if and how to put the new product into full-scale introduction. Test marketing is a learning experience. Analyze the results to find out about prospects and customer behavior. As well as measuring new product performance, use the test marketing phase to evaluate the efficiency of manufacturing, distribution, stock control, and sales systems. This is the last chance to see that nothing has been overlooked before the major launch.

Market Testing

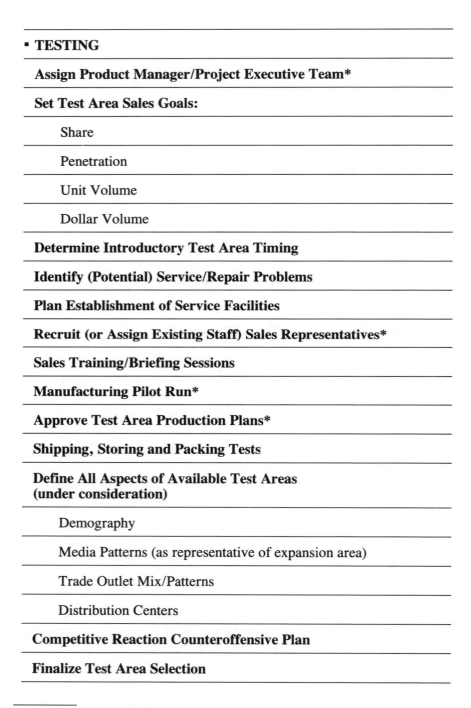

- **TESTING**

  Assign Product Manager/Project Executive Team*

  Set Test Area Sales Goals:

    Share

    Penetration

    Unit Volume

    Dollar Volume

  Determine Introductory Test Area Timing

  Identify (Potential) Service/Repair Problems

  Plan Establishment of Service Facilities

  Recruit (or Assign Existing Staff) Sales Representatives*

  Sales Training/Briefing Sessions

  Manufacturing Pilot Run*

  Approve Test Area Production Plans*

  Shipping, Storing and Packing Tests

  **Define All Aspects of Available Test Areas
  (under consideration)**

    Demography

    Media Patterns (as representative of expansion area)

    Trade Outlet Mix/Patterns

    Distribution Centers

  Competitive Reaction Counteroffensive Plan

  Finalize Test Area Selection

* Top management action/decision required

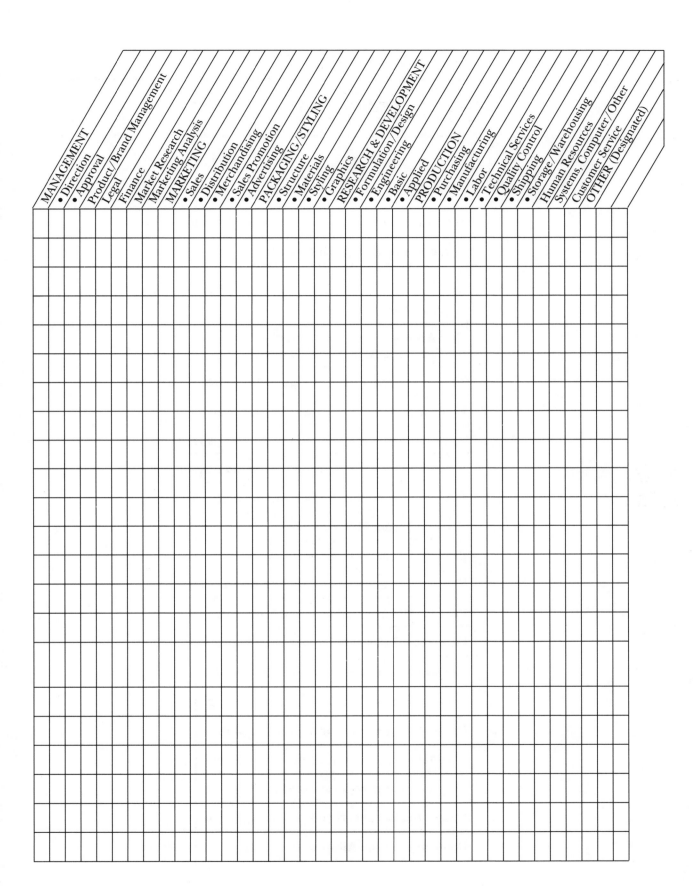

Set Test Area Goals, Unit and Dollar Volume
Forecast Profit/Loss Limits of:*
Successful Venture
Unsuccessful Write-off
Test Area Simulation of National (or Full Expansion Area) Plan
Test Area Media Plan (in line with expansion objectives)
Determine Test Area Total Appropriation*
Approve Test Area Advertising Materials (end-user)
Approve Trade Advertising/Merchandising Materials
Determine Merchandising Plan and Appropriation
Prepare Media Merchandising
Prepare Trade Selling Sheets
Determine Educational Plan and Appropriation
Prepare Prospect Educational Materials
Determine PR/Publicity Plan and Appropriation
Prepare Introductory Publicity Materials
Determine Sales Promotion Plan and Appropriation
Devise Prospect Incentives, if/as required:
Premiums, Contests, Price Offers, Couponing, etc.
Consider Multiple/Associated Product Tie-ins
Determine Cooperative Advertising Policies
Determine Trade Allowance, Stocking Charge Policies

* Top management action/decision required

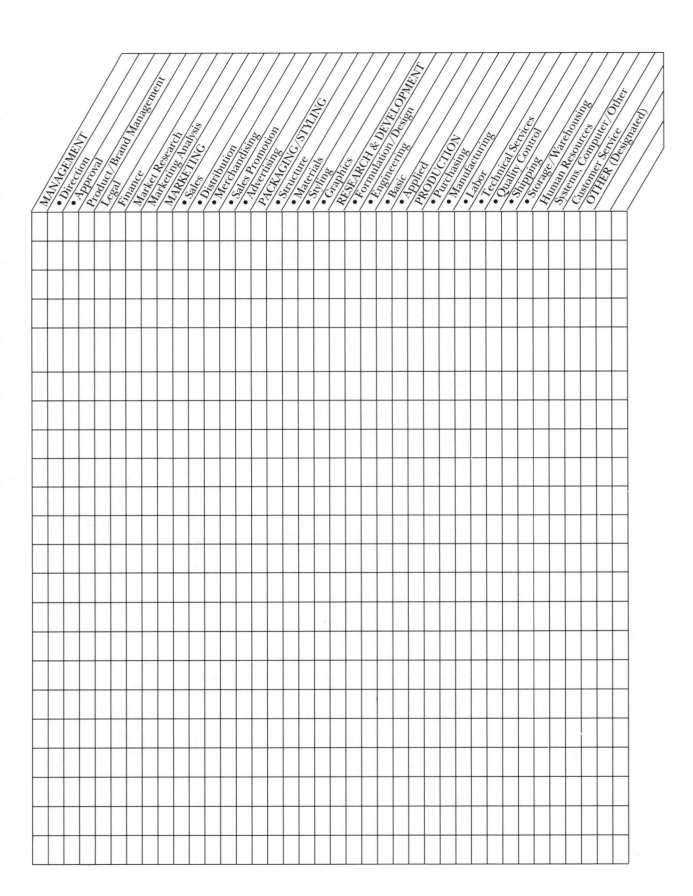

Prepare Cooperative Ads

Prepare Point-of-Purchase Materials

Hang-tags, Boots, Self-Displays

Determine Trade Sampling Appropriation, Program

Approve Test Area Commercial and Print Insertion Schedule

Contract Insurance Coverage for Test Area Product Indemnity

Set Sales Quotas

Devise Sales Incentives, Bonuses, Premiums for Sales Force

Set Introductory Trade Incentives, Buying Allowances, Contests, Celebrations, Celebrity Visits, etc.

Sign-off on Product Printed (support) Materials

Set-up Test Area User-Purchased Audit Panel

Execute Trade Sales Kick-off

Pre-introductory Measure of Brand Name Awareness (as compared with total universe awareness)

Advertising Kick-off

Survey of Trade Performance in Test Area

Test Area User Research

Media Coverage and Intensity Progress Reports in Test Area

Adjust Schedule to Meet Plan

Post-introductory Measure of Brand Name/Product Awareness

Post-introductory New Product Profile Study

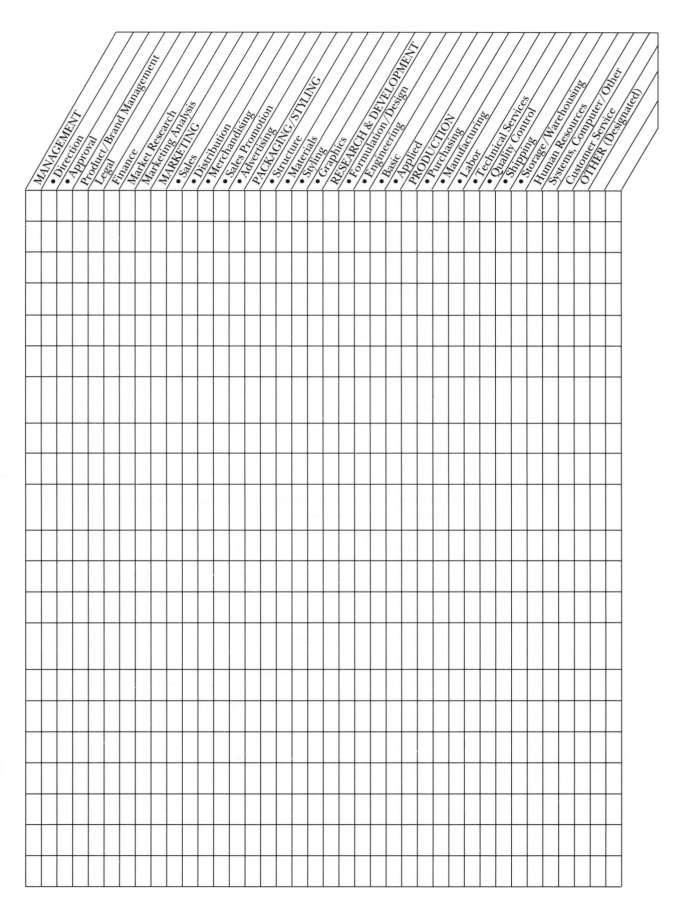

Analyze Factory Sales Data from Test Area
Program Performance Reports in Test Area:
Adjust to Meet Standards/Goals
Competitive Media/Trade Incentive/Special Promotions
Trend Report in Test Area
Evaluation of Sales and Advertising Effectiveness:
via Progress Reports throughout Area
Test Timetable
Wrap-up Test Area Performance Evaluation
Define Special Line Management Attention or Policy Changes Required in Large Scale Roll-Out*
Updated Budget Forecast
▪ **REQUEST APPROVAL FOR MAJOR EXPANSION**
▪ **DECISION***
GO—Move on to next phase
GO—Extend/Enlarge/Embellish/Accelerate
GO—Modify, as Specified (time, budget, staff, etc.)
NO GO—Abort
NO GO—Pursue Substitute Opportunity
NO GO—Modify, as Specified

* Top management action/decision required

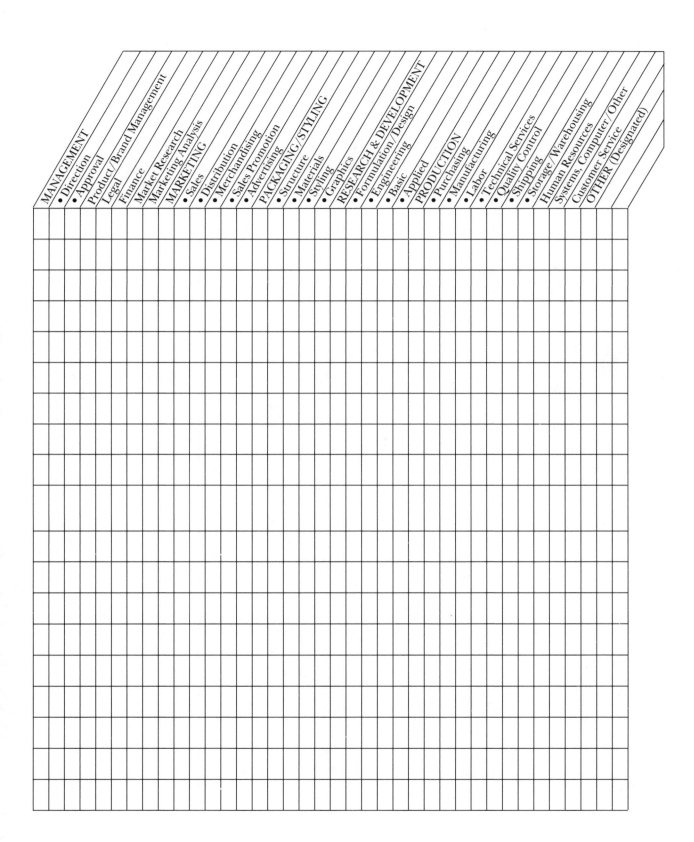

Major Introduction

Test marketing has given you an indication of how successful your new product introduction is likely to be. You have made all the necessary adjustments to product, packaging, the distribution system, and marketing plans and sales forecasts. You are ready for a full-scale product introduction.

ASSESSMENT AND EXPANSION

Checklist 7.1, the last checklist in the book, concentrates on evaluating performance and planning follow-up products to support the successful new introduction. The checklist outlines a program for assessment and expansion.

The checklist suggests various methods to measure the success of the new product: advertising response, telephone surveys, point-of-sale audits, talking to customers, and talking to sales channels. It is important to talk to everyone involved in the process, from factory to user. Make sure that research and evaluation continue well after the product has been launched—implement periodic checks.

As well as monitoring overall performance in the roll-out areas, pay particular attention to the original test markets. Because the product was introduced here first, it is likely that signs of decline, competitive actions, or new customer needs will show here earlier than in later expansion areas.

It is essential, too, to keep track of the competition. Successful follow-up products rely on anticipating and meeting competitive moves. To establish a dominant new product or brand, you need to keep competitors out of the market for as long as possible.

The second section of Checklist 7.1 focuses on plans for leveraging from new product success, through expanding the product line. A successful introduction opens new doors, and the new product development cycle begins again.

Major Introduction

- **APPROVE UPDATED BUDGET FORECAST***

- **ASSIGN TO APPROPRIATE REVENUE DIVISION, OR ESTABLISH NEW ONE***

- **ASSIGN APPROPRIATE PRODUCT MANAGEMENT***

- **ASSESSMENT**

Review Original New Product Objectives

Review New Product Development System

Measure Performance

Advertising Response

Telephone Surveys

Point-of-Sales Audits

Reports from Customers

Reports from Sales Channels

Establish Periodic Review Program

Monitor Test Markets

Assess Competition

Exploit Competitive Weaknesses Revealed by New Success

Identify and Exploit Unaddressed New Niches

Seal off New Niches from Potential Competition

Implement Plan to Limit Competition Encroachments

* Top management action/decision required

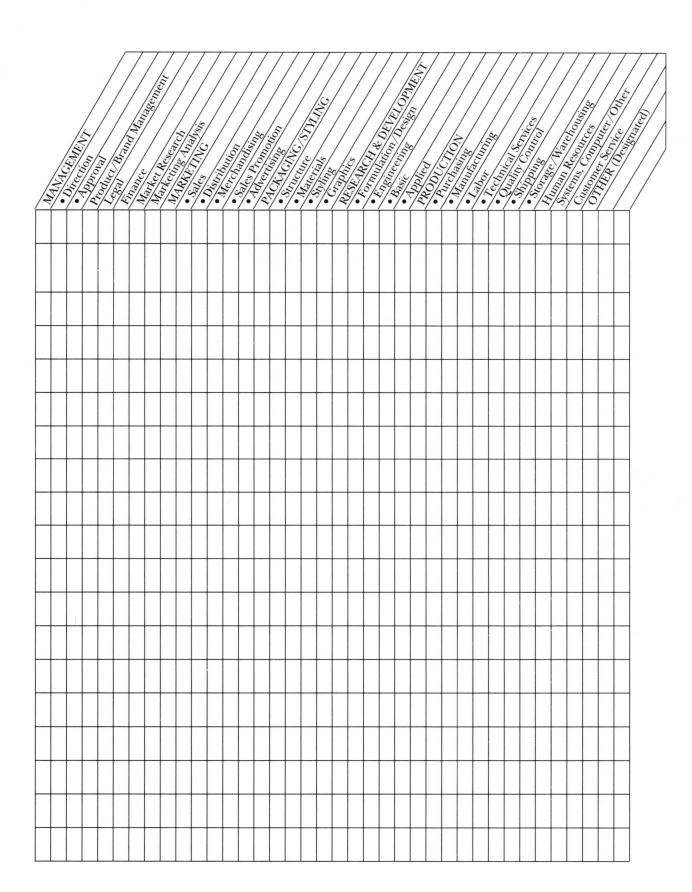

▪ EXPANSION

Implement Plan for Leveraging Success

Increase Production Capacity

Explore New Knowledge/Technology That the Development Program Has Opened Up

Develop Line Extensions

Develop Flankers

License Potential Other Industry, Related Products

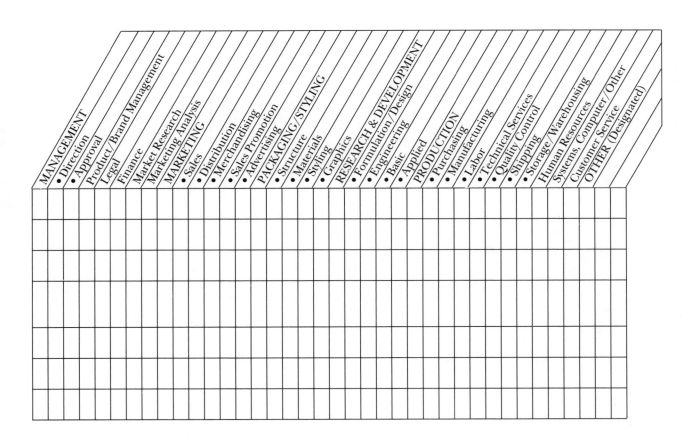

Afterword

No system, no research, no judgmental wisdom can assure success every time—even the most revolutionary scientific theory and conceptual artistic achievements may not be accepted when they are introduced. That's factual history.

What is also factual is that attending to all the details step-by-step, and constantly reviewing past steps and missteps as the program moves along, can help prevent costly surprises. That's the chief function of a checklist. Use it to plan—and use it to review past planning and actions.

This checklist system has been used in a variety of businesses as an aid in the total development of both products and services. It is broad-based enough to be easily modified to fit your own industry, trade and specific needs—as has been proven by its use literally hundreds of times.

Its review value is proven in use when examining reasons for premature success, early failure, so-so introductory results—and all the nuances between. Often the checklist review can pin down details to enhance success or to fix failure.

Its detailed nature helps lead to speed-ups, slow-downs and kills—the best utilization of your resources at the earliest phases of the process. Early kills can release funds for possible successes or early successes. Even the down side of the checklist system has virtues.

The new product adventure is a wedding of innovation and marketing—the most challenging, exciting and rewarding combination in business.

Every aspect calls on your creativity—the assembly of knowledge and its rearrangement in an original, compelling manner.

With checklist in hand, go forth to create and to enhance future successes.

ABOUT THE AUTHOR

George Gruenwald is a corporate growth and development consultant specializing in the identification and hands-on implementation of new business and new products opportunities for many of the world's largest corporations.

From 1972 to 1984, he was successively president, chairman, chief executive and chief creative officer of Campbell-Mithun, Inc. (now Campbell-Mithun-Esty), a major advertising agency with an international reputation for successful new products marketing development. Mr. Gruenwald has worked in the subject field of this book with more than 25 Fortune 500 corporations.

Previously, Mr. Gruenwald was founder and chief executive of Pilot Products, Inc., a new products marketing development service; Advance Brands, Inc., a sales and distribution service; and was a founding officer of North Advertising Incorporated (now Grey Advertising). Earlier, he was a new products brand and advertising manager at Gillette's Personal Care division; creative director at Willys-Overland Motors (now Chrysler's Jeep division), and assistant to the president of UARCO Incorporated.

Mr. Gruenwald frequently speaks on new products for private industry, trade and professional associations and universities. He is a new products columnist for the American Marketing Association's *Marketing News*, author of *New Product Development*, a comprehensive business text, and the subject of a 1989 business video interview of the same title, in which he shares his "Seven Steps to Success" in developing and launching new products and services.

Recently, Mr. Gruenwald was a corresponding task group member of the "Engineering Stages of New Product Development," a cooperative effort of the National Institute of Standards and Technology and the National Society of Professional Engineers, under which inventors and small businesses may receive technical and financial support to bring their energy-saving ideas to market.[1] (An inventor, Mr. Gruenwald holds the Venture Group® trademark).[2]

---

1. The NIST/NSPE definitions were to be applied in the operation, management and evaluation of the Department of Energy/National Institute of Standards and Technology (DOE/NIST) Energy-Related Inventions Program (ERIP).
2. Registered Service Trademark U.S. Patent Office 920358.

A long-time member of the Public Broadcasting Service (PBS) board, Mr. Gruenwald has headed committees and task forces on Future Service Opportunities and on Technology Applications. His interests in nutrition and health led to his election as a trustee of the Linus Pauling Institute of Science and Medicine and as a director of the American Institute of Wine & Food, which is dedicated to related educational and archival interests.

During World War II, he was a public relations writer and editor for the allied air forces in the Mediterranean theater of operations. He has a bachelor of science degree from Northwestern University's Medill School of Journalism, and attended the Chicago Academy of Fine Arts.

TITLES OF INTEREST IN
MARKETING AND SALES PROMOTION
FROM NTC BUSINESS BOOKS

Contact: 4255 West Touhy Avenue
Lincolnwood, IL 60646-1975
800-323-4900 (in Illinois, 708-679-5500)

SUCCESSFUL DIRECT MARKETING METHODS, Fourth Edition, by Bob Stone

PROFITABLE DIRECT MARKETING by Jim Kobs

READINGS AND CASES IN DIRECT MARKETING by Herb Brown and Bruce Buskirk

SUCCESSFUL TELEMARKETING by Bob Stone and John Wyman

HOW TO CREATE SUCCESSFUL CATALOGS by Maxwell Sroge

BEST SALES PROMOTIONS, Sixth Edition, by William A. Robinson

INSIDE THE LEADING MAIL ORDER HOUSES, Third Edition, by Maxwell Sroge

NEW PRODUCT DEVELOPMENT by George Gruenwald

THE COMPLETE TRAVEL MARKETING HANDBOOK by Andrew Vladimir

HOW TO TURN CUSTOMER SERVICE INTO CUSTOMER SALES by Bernard Katz

THE MARKETING PLAN by Robert K. Skacel

ADVERTISING & MARKETING CHECKLISTS by Ron Kaatz

SECRETS OF SUCCESSFUL DIRECT MAIL by Richard V. Benson

U.S. DEPARTMENT OF COMMERCE GUIDE TO EXPORTING

HOW TO GET PEOPLE TO DO THINGS YOUR WAY by J. Robert Parkinson

HOW TO WRITE A SUCCESSFUL MARKETING PLAN by Roman G. Hiebing, Jr., and Scott W. Cooper

101 TIPS FOR MORE PROFITABLE CATALOGS by Maxwell Sroge

HOW TO GET THE MOST OUT OF TRADE SHOWS by Steve Miller

MARKETING TO CHINA by Xu Bai Yi

STRATEGIC MARKET PLANNING by Robert J. Hamper and L. Sue Baugh

COMMONSENSE DIRECT MARKETING, Second Edition, by Drayton Bird

NTC'S DICTIONARY OF MAILING LIST TERMINOLOGY AND TECHNIQUES by Nat G. Bodian